Firstfruits
God's Plan for Your Success

PASTOR BARRY S. WASHINGTON, SR.

DIAKONIA PUBLISHING
GREENSBORO, NORTH CAROLINA

Firstfruits

published by Diakonia Publishing

Copyright © 2008 by Barry S. Washington, Sr.

ISBN: 978-0-9800877-2-7

Cover and book design by Jeff Pate

Unless otherwise noted, Scripture references and quotations were taken from THE HOLY BIBLE, Authorized King James Version, containing the Old and New Testaments. Published by Thomas Nelson, Inc. © Copyright 1970.

No part of this publication may be reproduced, stored in a retrieval system, or transmitted, in any form or by any means—electronic, mechanical, photocopying, recording or otherwise—without prior written permission.

For Information:
DIAKONIA PUBLISHING
P.O. Box 9512
Greensboro, North Carolina 27429-0512
www.ephesians412.net

Or you may contact the author by writing to:
Whole Man Ministries
P.O. Box 21173
Winston-Salem, NC 27120
www.wholemanminstries.com

Contents

	Foreword by Dr. James C. Hash Sr.	5
1	God's Plan For Your Success	7
2	What is the Firstfruits?	14
3	The Power to Get Wealth	28
4	The Curse Has Been Reversed	38
5	Place a Demand on Heaven	62
6	From Rags to Riches: The Story of Jacob	77
7	Sowing and Reaping	85
8	Key to Answered Prayers	104
9	How Do I Change My Situation?	117

Appendix:

I'm a 100% Tither	139
Are You Being a Good Steward?	139
Where Does the Tithe Go?	140

This book is dedicated to my mother Juliette Marie Baldwin, who taught me to believe there is a "silver lining" behind every dark cloud. She is my hero, my mentor, and my greatest teacher. Love ya, Mama.

To my wife Camilla F. Washington, who keeps me in perfect harmony.

Last but not least, to the members of Whole Man Ministries, who believe in not despising small beginnings.

Special thanks to those who have assisted me: Mr. Tillerson, Dr. Hash, Pastor King, Rev. Patton, Ms. Breathette, Min. Wyatt, and others. With their assistance, special consideration was taken to bring forth *Firstfruits*, wherein I am indebted to their kindness.

foreword

How should our tithes be used? Who should we give our money to? How does God measure our giving? Does God care about our debt? What happens when we give? How do we earn a heavenly reward? These are questions that run through the minds of both the Christian and the non-Christian.

With the challenging subject of tithing, Pastor Washington shows in ***Firstfruits:** God's Plan for Your Success* that Jesus taught more about money than any other topic except the kingdom of God.

With the combinations of being biblically based thinkers, level-headed, faith-inspired, and practical planners you will find in this book keys to basic sound financial management. Reading ***Firstfruits*** will help you to function biblically, and give faithfully to reap God's harvest joyfully.

Dr. James C. Hash, Sr.
Pastor, St. Peter's World Outreach Center
Winston-Salem, NC

chapter 1

God's Plan for Your Success

This book of the law shall not depart out of thy mouth; but thou shalt meditate therein day and night, that thou mayest observe to do according to all that is written therein: for then thou shalt make thy way prosperous, and then thou shalt have good success. [Joshua 1:8]

As the passage above states, it is God's will that our lives be successful and prosperous. In this book I want to stress that God honors your firstfruit, and as a result He rewards you with abundance. Therefore, the principles taught in the following pages will help people succeed in all their endeavors. It's my belief that God's plan is to make us succeed if we offer HIM our firstfruit.

If I told you about an investment where you would get a guaranteed return on the money you invested—would you want to be in on it? If I told you that you could invest 10% or more of your income and receive monthly dividend checks of three, six, or even ten times your investment, would you participate?

Firstfruits is a form of tithing—a way to honor God simply because of who He is. When we offer our firstfruits to God, we are expressing our faith and appreciation for what He has given us. Giving the firstfruits is making an investment into the kingdom of God that produces future dividends that are guaranteed by God. Not only do you benefit others through the firstfruits, but you also reap the benefits from what you are investing. What a great deal!

I'll say this from the beginning because many have taught the same principles I will teach in this book from a position of fear. If you don't give the firstfruits or tithe, it doesn't mean that God is angry with you, or that your position as a child of God is in jeopardy. Just because you don't give or tithe will NOT keep you out of Heaven. However, God's grace is filled with so many benefits in this present world, and many of these benefits are activated through trusting God in the area of giving the firstfruits. God wants you to enjoy your life, and He is glorified when His children are blessed. So why not partake of all His goodness?

Have you ever considered driving without automobile insurance? Has the thought crossed your mind to accept full-time employment without any health care benefits? Or would you purchase a home without homeowners insurance that protects your home against unseen dangers such as floods, tornadoes, fire, or damaging winds? When we don't give the firstfruits we open ourselves to these risks. No one can insure your property or protect your interests like God. While insurance in the natural protects *against* loss, His insurance protects *from* loss. It's a sure bet that you can't lose.

We insure practically everything we own, from homes to the jewelry we wear. Firstfruits is the greatest insurance and investment a person can ever own because God places upon it His own seal of approval.

Many of us who are beneficiaries of various policies seldom read the fine print. The same is true with the firstfruits: we don't familiarize ourselves with the benefits it provides us. This is what I want to accomplish through this book. Many are writing about all the negatives and curses associated with the tithe, but I want to convey to you the benefits.

We will review the accounts of several patriarchs of the faith who brought the firstfruits of their increase to God: Abel, Abraham, Jacob, David, Solomon, and others. Furthermore, we will see that the apostle Paul sanctioned the practice of the firstfruits in the church, as well as Jesus Himself endorsing the tithe as something we "ought" to do.

The Bible says that the firstfruit of our increase is what God desires from us (Proverbs 3:9). God has entrusted us to give back to Him as an expression of faith, honor, and appreciation for all He does for us. The first 10% is God's and He allows us to be stewards over the remaining 90%. For example, if you receive $100, you should honor God with the first $10.00. Remember this, your tithe is a way to thank God for the many blessings He provides for you. The tithe is for your benefit and the benefit of others—not God. God doesn't need your money, but He has established a system whereby He can open up the windows of heaven and pour out a blessing in your life (Malachi 3:10).

God has established that a person who tithes will reap the benefits of their seed sown. The Bible says, *Honor the LORD with thy substance and with the first fruit of all thine increase, so shall thy barns be filled with plenty and thy presses shall burst with new wine.* [Proverbs 3:9-10]

God guarantees that our barns would be filled, an expression of material prosperity at the expense of giving God His portion—the firstfruits.

When we do not give the firstfruits of our increase, we are saying that we don't believe the system God has established—we don't believe His word. Instead, when we do not tithe, we are saying that we trust in ourselves, our abilities, our jobs, and God becomes second. The opposite is true when we do. We invest in the building of God's kingdom; in future ministers and ministries and other workers in His vineyard. Our God is able to pay dividends beyond our imagination. He even places His reputation on the line when He said, *Bring ye all the tithes into the storehouse, that there may be meat in mine house, and prove me now herewith, saith the LORD of hosts, if I will not open you the windows of heaven, and pour you out a blessing, that there shall be not room enough to receive it.* [Malachi 3:10]

As kids we would put sticks upon our shoulders and dared someone to knock it off; or we would draw a circle in the sand around us and dare anyone to cross the line. If someone violated any of these commands, we were forced to follow up with action, because our reputation was on the line. The same is true with God concerning the firstfruits. God has issued a challenge to each of us; and put

His reputation on the line. Break the line of God's circle, knock off His stick, and God is forced to follow with action. "Prove me now, saith the LORD!" God cannot lie and He is always faithful to His word. You are not manipulating God with your tithe, you are simply taking God at His word.

Some of you may object to this by thinking that the tithe is an Old Testament requirement. Some of you may also ask, "Is tithing a New Testament principle?" Yes and no. The tithe is a spiritual law that was established before the law of Moses in the Old Testament. Tithing was practiced from the beginning with Cain and Abel, and then through Abraham, which was 430 years before the law was given; and was later made part of the law of Moses.

Tithing was also practiced by the churches in the New Testament. In 1 Corinthians 16:2 says, *Upon the first [day] of the week let every one of you lay by him in store, as [God] hath prospered him, that there be no gatherings when I come.*

Jesus even said that we ought to tithe. In Matthew 23:23, the Lord was scolding the scribes and Pharisees, *Woe unto you, scribes and Pharisees, hypocrites! For ye pay tithe of mint and anise and cummin, and have omitted the weightier [matters] of the law, judgment, mercy, and faith.* ***These ought ye to have done, and not to leave the other undone***. Jesus said that we ought to tithe, but not leave the other (judgment, mercy, and faith), undone. In fact, as you will learn in this book, the two go hand in hand when understood properly.

Don't continue to miss out on the blessings God has in store for you. Give Him your firstfruits, and get ready to receive blessings you won't have enough room to receive. If you apply the principles taught in this book, you too shall find your barns filled with plenty, and your presses bursting out with new wine. Trust God and He shall bring you through to victory.

> **Did You Know?**
>
> **God guarantees that our barns would be filled, an expression of material prosperity at the expense of giving God His portion—the firstfruits.**

chapter 2
What is the Firstfruits?

Honour the LORD with thy substance, and with the firstfruits of all thine increase: So shall thy barns be filled with plenty, and thy presses shall burst out with new wine. [Proverbs 3:9-10]

In the beginning, God gave Adam complete dominion over everything in the earth. He had authority over all creation—every tree, animal, bird, fish, and insect. He was, in essence, a god over the earth. However, in all this power and authority, God gave him just one restriction. He told Adam that he could eat of every tree in the garden, but one—and that tree was the Tree of the Knowledge of Good and Evil. How many of you know that with power and authority comes responsibility? I believe this is the first example of the principle of honoring God with the firstfruits. The Bible says that the firstfruits is a form of tithing and belongs to God. Exodus 23:19 says, *The first of the firstfruits of thy land thou shalt bring into the house of the LORD thy God.*

The firstfruits is the very best we have to offer God—it's the first, not the second or the third, but the first. God deserves the very best we have to offer, and He should be first. It is a way of saying we honor and worship you as the Scripture says, *Honour the LORD with thy substance, and with the firstfruits of all thine increase.* [Proverbs 3:9]

Now where does the Bible tell us to bring the firstfruits? The prophet Nehemiah gives us the answer, *And to bring the firstfruits of our ground, and the firstfruits of all fruit of all trees, year by year, unto the house of the LORD... unto the priests that minister in the house of our God.* [Nehemiah 10:35-36]

Leviticus 27:30 says, *And all the tithe of the land, whether of the seed of the land, or of the fruit of the land, or of the fruit of the tree, is the LORD'S: it is holy unto the LORD.*

We see that God had given Adam a great majority of the garden, but retained the remaining one tree as holy unto the Lord. We also know that Adam disobeyed this command and ate from the tree, which released the curse into the earth. Adam took what God had reserved for Himself.

As it was in the beginning, so it is today when one doesn't honor God's portion—the tithe—the curse is released. I will stress again that this doesn't mean that God is angry or that a Christian is no longer in right standing with God. When I say, "the curse is released," I am referring to a spiritual law that God put into place when He created the world. God said, *I call heaven and earth to record this day against you, that I have set before you life and death, blessing and cursing: therefore choose life, that both thou and thy seed may live.* [Deuteronomy 30:19]

> **Did You Know?**
>
> When we believe that our wealth and successes have come as a result of our own strength and wisdom, we find it very difficult to honor God in this way.

Because of this spiritual law, God has given us the choice to have life or death, blessing or cursing. He even gives us the answer (*choose life*), but still, it is our choice—not God's; and since God cannot take back His word, He honors the choices we make.

Because the firstfruits belong to God and is holy, everyone who honors God by bringing their tithe to Him shall reap the benefits of His blessings. Bringing the firstfruits honors a God who *is able to supply all your need according to his riches in glory by Christ Jesus* (Philippians 4:19), who is also able to unleash the continuous power of Heaven upon you, a God who possesses unlimited resources that are not dependent on the world's economy, or bound by famine or drought.

So what does it mean to bring God the firstfruits of all our increase? In order to answer that question, we must first have the correct perception. We must understand that the earth and everything therein belongs to God (Psalm 24:1). Every good and perfect gift is from above and comes from the Father in Heaven (James 1:17). When we come into agreement with the truth that everything we own or accomplish is by God's grace, mercy, and blessing, we can then find it easy to honor Him with the first portion of our increase—the firstfruits.

On the other hand, when we believe that our wealth and successes have come as a result of our own strength and wisdom, we find it very difficult to honor God in this way. God spoke through the prophet Jeremiah

> **Tithing Tips**
>
> Fruit alone is not acceptable to God. He desires the firstfruits of your increase because it shows Him that your faith is perfect concerning His promises of prosperity.

concerning this:

Thus saith the LORD; Cursed be the man that trusteth in man, and maketh flesh his arm, and whose heart departeth from the LORD. For he shall be like the heath in the desert, and shall not see when good cometh; but shall inhabit the parched places in the wilderness, in a salt land and not inhabited. Blessed is the man that trusteth in the LORD, and whose hope the LORD is. For he shall be as a tree planted by the waters, and that spreadeth out her roots by the river, and shall not see when heat cometh, but her leaf shall be green; and shall not be careful in the year of drought, neither shall cease from yielding fruit. [Jeremiah 17:5-8]

It is clear from the mouth of God that trusting in Him releases His blessings in your life. When you bring the firstfruits to God, you are acknowledging that God is Jehovah-Jireh, the Lord who provides (Genesis 22:14). Additionally, you are conveying faith and thanksgiving for His grace and blessing.

What then is the firstfruits? According to the Bible, the firstfruit is the first portion of your ripe harvest: the best of your oil, the best of your wheat, the best of your sheep, oxen, the best of your wages. It is the tithe—God's portion (Exodus 22:29; Numbers 18:12).

The firstfruits is the portion that you return to God as a way to honor His name for the furtherance of His kingdom. We call this kingdom building. As I stated before, it's our perception that counts—how we view the benefits we enjoy on a daily basis. Did we acquire our wealth, health, homes, cars, jobs without the benefit of God's grace and mercy? Or were they acquired through our own power?

God was quick to forewarn the children of Israel of this once He brought them into the Promised Land.

For the LORD thy God bringeth thee into a good land, a land of brooks of water, of fountains and depths that spring out of valleys and hills; a land of wheat, and barley, and vines, and fig trees, and pomegranates; a land of oil olive, and honey; a land wherein thou shalt eat bread without scarceness, thou shalt not lack any thing in it; a land whose stones are iron, and out of whose hills thou mayest dig brass.

When thou hast eaten and art full, then thou shalt bless the LORD thy God for the good land which he hath given thee. Beware that thou forget not the LORD thy God, in not keeping his commandments, and his judgments, and his statutes, which I command thee this day: Lest when thou hast eaten and art full, and hast built goodly houses, and dwelt therein; and when thy herds and thy flocks multiply, and thy silver and thy gold is multiplied, and all that thou hast is multiplied; Then thine heart be lifted up, and thou forget the LORD thy God, which brought thee forth out of the land of Egypt, from the house of bondage; Who led thee through that great and terrible wilderness, wherein were fiery serpents, and scorpions, and drought, where there was no water; who brought thee forth water out of the rock of flint; Who fed thee in the wilderness with manna, which thy fathers knew not, that he might humble thee, and that he might prove thee, to do thee good at thy latter end; and thou say in thine heart, My power and the might of mine hand hath gotten me this wealth. But thou shalt remember the LORD thy God: for it is he that giveth thee power to get wealth, that he may establish his covenant which he sware unto thy fathers, as it is this day.

And it shall be, if thou do at all forget the LORD thy God, and walk after other gods, and serve them, and worship them, I testify against you this day that ye shall surely perish. As the nations which the LORD destroyeth before your face, so shall ye perish; because ye would not be obedient unto the voice of the LORD your God. [Deuteronomy 8:7-20]

In comparison to our lives, He too has brought us out of Egypt and through the wilderness of a cruel world. He fed us, clothed us, and delivered us from a life of bondage. Whether we found ourselves in the prisons of debt, drugs, sicknesses, or broken relationships, it is God's grace that has pulled us through.

As God stated, *For it is he that giveth thee power to get wealth, that he may establish his covenant which he sware unto thy fathers,* God has a purpose in making you prosperous. First and foremost, God wants you prosperous because He loves you. Secondly, prosperity in your life reflects the covenant God has made with us in Christ, *that,* as the Scripture says, *the blessing of Abraham would come upon the Gentiles through Jesus Christ* (Galatians 3:14).

God gives you the power to be prosperous and enjoy the fruits of your labor, while at the same time, requiring you to give Him a portion to establish and continue His work in the world. It is God who gives you the power to get this wealth. Even Solomon, the wisest man of his time, knew the importance of honoring God with his substance, and the firstfruits of his increase (Proverbs 3:9).

We all should want to honor God; and we can do so

by giving Him a portion of what He has already given us. Your firstfruits unto God contributes to two things. First and foremost, it supports the spreading of the gospel: the spiritual feeding of God's people, the saving of souls, the healing of sicknesses and disease, the development of future ministers and so on.

Secondly, offering your firstfruits unto God represents that you trust God for your prosperity. The Bible says, *And so shall thy barns be filled with plenty*. God promises that by honoring Him with the firstfruits, he will open up the windows of heaven and pour out a blessing that we will not have room enough to receive it (Malachi 3:10). As we bring our firstfruits unto God, we have the right to expect His blessing to be released in return.

The offering of firstfruits does not "buy" God's blessing. We cannot earn God's grace. Otherwise, it would not be grace, but works (Romans 11:6). By giving God back the first portion of our increase, we are acting upon God's promises that He has blessed us with all spiritual blessings in heavenly places in Christ (Ephesians 1:6). This is faith in action and as the Bible says, *For as the body without the spirit is dead, so then faith without works is dead also.* [James 2:26]

We must be doers of the word and not hearers only.

The Bible says that if we only hear this word concerning the firstfruits, and do not act upon it, we are deceiving ourselves (James 1:22-23).

There are several examples recorded in the Bible that give us illustrations of the firstfruits. The first example we have in Scripture is from Adam and Eve while the second comes from Cain and Abel and their offering to the Lord. We can see by Cain and Abel's actions, that their parents (or God Himself) had taught them the principles of sacrifices and offerings. Both brothers brought an offering to God, but only Abel's was accepted.

Why was Abel's offering accepted and Cain's not? The Bible says, **By faith** *Abel offered unto God a more excellent sacrifice than Cain, by which he obtained witness that he was righteous, God testifying of his gifts: and by it he being dead yet speaketh.* [Hebrews 11:4]

We see now that God was and has always dealt with man according to faith; and as the Scripture teaches that Abel's faith brought about his works, and by works his faith was made perfect (James 2:22).

And in process of time it came to pass, that Cain brought of the fruit of the ground an offering unto the LORD. And Abel, he also brought of the firstlings of his flock and of the fat thereof. And the LORD had respect unto Abel and to his offering: But unto Cain and to his offering he had not respect. And Cain was very wroth, and his countenance fell. And the LORD said unto Cain, Why art thou wroth? and why is thy countenance fallen? If thou doest well, shalt thou not be accepted? and if thou doest not well, sin lieth at the door. And unto thee shall be his desire, and thou shalt rule over him. [Genesis 4:3-6]

We see that Cain brought *of the fruit of the ground* as an offering, while Abel brought the *firstlings of his flock*. The term "firstling" is from the Hebrew word $b^e k\hat{o}r\hat{a}h$ meaning the "firstling of a man or beast; birthright, firstborn" (Strong's Concordance). In essence, Abel offered unto God what was eventually required by the law in Exodus 13:12-13, which was to bring the firstborn of every beast to the Lord. This served two redemptive purposes under the law. The first was to atone for sins and to restore fellowship with God; and the second was a way of honoring God.

Genesis.4:3-4 clearly highlights the truth of firstfruits. Cain, the first son of Adam and Eve, only brought the fruit of the ground, but his younger brother Abel brought the firstlings of his flock. The Bible says God honored Abel's offering but rejected Cain's. It is clear that God demands the very first of all of our increase. The tithe belongs to the Lord, also the very first of all He allows as increase in our lives.

Now we know that we no longer have to bring sacrifices to atone for our sins because of the perfect sacrifice of Jesus. Our sins are forgiven and we are in relationship with God based solely on what Jesus did. However, as I said before, bringing the firstfruits is a way to honor God for all His blessings.

In respect to Cain's offering, we know that the Scripture refers to Abel's offering as being "more excellent" than Cain's because of faith. Therefore, we must conclude the reason God was not pleased with Cain's offering was because Cain had not mixed faith in it; and this was revealed in the fact that he brought only the fruit of the ground as an offering. Since the Scripture does not specifically mention Cain's offering to be the firstfruits, but yet it does with Abel's, we can rightly conclude that Cain's faith was not perfect by his works. If it had been, Cain would have brought the first portion of his harvest, along with a blood sacrifice, as an act of faith.

Let us look also at God's response to Cain. When Cain understood that God was not pleased with his offering, he was angry. God was not the one who was angry; it was Cain. God engaged Cain to restore fellowship with him—not the other way around. Let us remember that it was Cain's *offering* for which God had not respect—not the person of Cain. God wasn't rejecting Cain. He wanted to let Cain know that he was still in relationship with Him, and said, *If thou doest well, shalt thou not be accepted? and if thou doest not well, sin lieth at the door. And unto thee shall be his desire, and thou shalt rule over him.*

BENEFITS

God will rebuke the devourer for your sake; and he will not destroy your fruits (Malachi 3:11).

The Lord was teaching Cain that if he would simply trust His ways, he would be accepted. But if not—when you don't trust God's ways, you open the door to sin and its death. Fruit alone is not acceptable to God. He desires the firstfruits of your increase because it shows Him that your faith is perfect concerning His promises of prosperity.

Throughout the Bible, the term "firstfruits" is used to describe a special dedication or blessing. For example, in the Old Testament, Israel is described as God's *firstfruits* (Jeremiah 2:3). Christ in His resurrection is also described as *the firstfruits of them that slept* (1 Corinthians 15:20). The people of God today (Christians) are also said to be *firstfruits* (Romans 16:5; 1

Corinthians 16:15; James 1:18) having received the *firstfruits* or earnest of the Spirit of God (Romans 8:23).

The Bible says that the Lord has given us the power to get wealth so that He may establish His covenant in the earth (Deuteronomy 8:18). In the next chapter, we will discuss what this means and how we are to use the principles of the firstfruits to activate the power God has given us to be wealthy.

chapter 3
The Power to Get Wealth

But thou shalt remember the LORD thy God, for it is he that giveth thee power to get wealth, that he may establish his covenant which he sware unto thy fathers, as it is this day. [Deuteronomy 8:18]

God has given us the power to get wealth. This power was given to us freely, by grace, so that His covenant may be established in the earth. Most Christians have issues with wealth because they have been taught that being a Christian is about being poor. This is a result of a misunderstanding of what wealth actually is, and why God wants us to be wealthy.

The purpose of becoming wealthy is to establish God's covenant, to be a witness in the land on behalf of Jesus Christ, to spread the gospel in more ways than one. We can see this in the words of Jesus when He said, *For I was an hungered, and ye gave me meat: I was thirsty, and ye gave me drink: I was a stranger, and ye took me in: Naked, and ye clothed me: I was sick, and ye visited me: I was in prison, and ye came unto me.* [Matthew 25:35-36]

True Wealth and Riches

Blessed is the man that feareth the LORD, that delighteth greatly in his commandments. His seed shall be mighty upon earth: the generation of the upright shall be blessed. Wealth and riches shall be in his house: and his righteousness endureth for ever.

Unto the upright there ariseth light in the darkness: he is gracious, and full of compassion, and righteous. A good man showeth favour, and lendeth: he will guide his affairs with discretion. [Psalm 112:1-5]

Wealth and riches can be defined in many ways. Being rich and wealthy isn't referring exclusively to money. The Bible speaks of many things being riches that have nothing to do with money. In fact, Jesus did not consider money to be an example of true riches. *If therefore ye have not been faithful in the unrighteous mammon, who will commit to your trust the true riches?* [Luke 16:11]

However, in terms of money, the Bible says that God has given us the power to get wealth, and promises wealth and riches to those that delight in His word and righteousness. Money is a resource that all of us need to operate in this world of ours. While most people acknowledge this, they also believe that money destroys people and relationships. So, in order to keep as far away from destruction, they prevent themselves from being wealthy in spite of God's promises.

We've all seen how people who grew up poor, when suddenly becoming rich, find themselves immersed in all kinds of trouble. Professional athletes seem to be the most profound victims. Many, after having been raised in poverty, go to college to play a sport and shortly thereafter find themselves signing a lucrative professional contract, which could possibly become a curse or a blessing, depending on the person and circumstances surrounding them. Often this is done because they want to "give back" to their families that have struggled over the years. Just as often as we see, suddenly becoming wealthy ends up being

> **Did You Know?**
>
> Money is not the root of all evil. The Bible says that the LOVE OF MONEY is.
>
> —1 Timothy 6:10

more destructive than poverty ever accomplished.

This is not the case for every professional player. Many are responsible and have given millions of dollars back to their communities in support of various programs. However, there are those who have yet to acknowledge that their true wealth comes from above.

We can also see this when people win the lottery. It is rare to find a lottery winner who is still wealthy. This is because this type of wealth is not profitable because it goes against a spiritual law. The Bible says, *Wealth gotten by vanity shall be diminished: but he that gathereth by labour shall increase.* [Proverbs 13:11]

When people say that money destroyed someone, they are not correct. Money does not destroy. It's the *love of money* that is so destructive. The Bible says, *For the love of money is the root of all evil: which while some coveted after, they have erred from the faith, and pierced themselves through with many sorrows.* [1 Timothy 6:10]

Money is good if it is used for a good purpose.

This is why God wants us to be wealthy and rich—not so we can boast of our own accomplishments, but so we can be a witness to what God has provided to make us wealthy. Let us remember, God's word does not say that He has given us wealth. Instead, it says that God has given us the power to get wealth; and what we do with that power determines our experience.

What is wealth then? Wealth is having the ability to help someone other than yourself. Wealth is owning two pairs of shoes above the pair you have. Wealth is measured in different ways—not only in monetary value or by the assets we possess, but by the life we live and the joy we have.

We can learn about this from Abraham. In Genesis 14, the Bible says that Abraham met Melchizedek after God had empowered him to defeat his enemies and rescue Lot and his belongings, and also all the goods that were taken from Sodom. After Melchizedek blessed Abraham, he remembered God by giving the priest of God Melchizedek the firstfruits of all the spoil of the victory. Abraham then demonstrated his trust in God by refusing to receive any of the goods he had returned to the king of Sodom.

And the king of Sodom said unto Abram, Give me the persons, and take the goods to thyself. And Abram said to the king of Sodom, I have lift up mine hand unto the LORD, the most high God, the possessor of heaven and earth, That I will not take from a thread even to a shoelatchet, and that I will not take any thing that is thine, lest thou shouldest say, I have made Abram rich. [Genesis 14:21-23]

Blessed to Be a Blessing

And I will make of thee a great nation, and I will bless thee, and make thy name great; and thou shalt be a blessing. [Genesis 12:2]

God has given us the power to get wealth so, as He said to Abraham, that we will be a blessing to others. The Lord never intended for us to store up wealth, build bigger houses, and accumulate unnecessary things to boost our honor among men. Owning bigger houses is not a sin in itself, but when we do

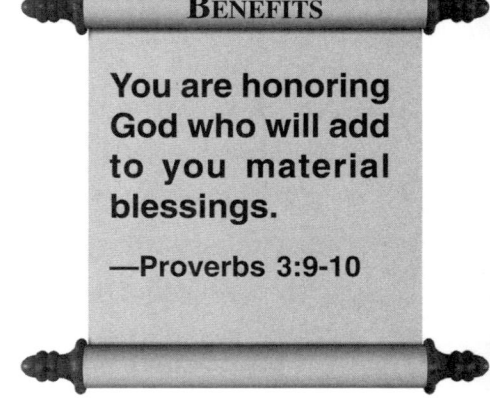

BENEFITS

You are honoring God who will add to you material blessings.

—Proverbs 3:9-10

these things to boost our honor among men it is. He desires that we become a living testimony of His goodness and generosity that began first with His Son Jesus, the greatest gift of all, and everything else He has given us that pertains to life and godliness.

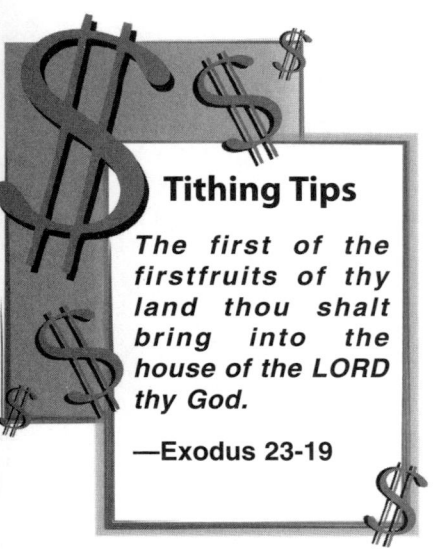

Tithing Tips

The first of the firstfruits of thy land thou shalt bring into the house of the LORD thy God.

—Exodus 23-19

As being wealthy is a witness of God's covenant, blessing others is more. God is the greatest giver of all, and what better way to represent Him than by giving—by being a blessing to others. This is what being wealthy is all about—amen?

Many people in this country see wealth as having a big house and fancy cars, and plenty of other stuff. Unfortunately, most of these "wealthy" people, along with all their stuff, have a bunch of debt to go along with it. They may have a lot of things and also may have a lot of money, but that is not true wealth.

Being wealthy means that you have excess in

order to give and help others who are in need—all without imposing on your finances. Paying your bills and debts is an effective witness for God. A truly wealthy person is as the Bible says, *Owe no man any thing, but to love one another: for he that loveth another hath fulfilled the law.* [Romans 13:8]

You may have a big house and fancy cars, and a big screen TV, but if you're so deep in debt that you can't help out a brother in need, then you are not wealthy. Do you see what I'm saying? God has blessed us so that we can be a blessing to others— to show them the love of God.

Proverbs 3:27-28 says, *Withhold not good from them to whom it is due, when it is in the power of thine hand to do it. Say not unto thy neighbour, Go, and come again, and to morrow I will give; when thou hast it by thee.*

There is a balance of "give and take"; and as long as you keep that balance, God does not mind you having a big house and fancy cars. Solomon was very rich and had many possessions until he lost his balance.

Harnessing the Power

Although God has given us the power to get wealth,

this power will not benefit us unless we learn how to use it properly. Everything God has given us is for our benefit and for the benefit of others. God has set up a system of using the power of God that seems to be abnormal according to man's ways. While the world teaches to accumulate wealth by saving and investing in the world's system, God's system teaches that wealth is accumulated by giving and investing in God's kingdom. While the world's wisdom is to store up treasure for yourselves, God's wisdom is to give in order that you may receive.

Jesus said, *So is he that layeth up treasure for himself, and is not rich toward God.* [Luke 12:21]

To the natural man, this seems foolish, but the Bible says, *But the natural man receiveth not the things of the Spirit of God: for they are foolishness unto him: neither can he know them, because they are spiritually discerned. But he that is spiritual judgeth all things, yet he himself is judged of no man.* [1 Corinthians 2:14-15]

The world's system is a broken system that provides only temporary benefits. God's kingdom provides benefits in this world and also in the world to come. God makes promises to the person who gives—that to the degree you give and the motivation behind your giving, your giving will be multiplied back to you. While the world's system is a system of addition, God's system is a system of multiplication. Wouldn't you rather have things multiplied in your life than added? Participate in God's system of unleashing the power to get wealth, and you will be blessed.

Jesus taught, *Give, and it shall be given unto you; good measure, pressed down, and shaken together, and running over, shall men give into your bosom. For with the same measure that ye mete withal it shall be measured to you again.* [Luke 6:38]

In the chapter "Sowing and Reaping" I will discuss the principles of giving in greater detail. This is the power that God has given to us—to be wealthy in order to demonstrate God's love to others through giving.

BENEFITS

For promotion cometh neither from the east, nor the west, nor from the south. But God is the judge. He putteth down one, and setteth up another.

—Psalm 75:6-7

chapter 4
The Curse Has Been Reversed

Christ hath redeemed us from the curse of the law, being made a curse for us: for it is written, Cursed is every one that hangeth on a tree. [Galatians 3:13]

The title of this chapter is "The Curse Has Been Reversed". That's what we need in our life. We need to know that the curse has been reversed so we can walk in the blessings of God. The problem is that many of us are walking around like we're cursed. God has given His word that tells us "the curse has been reversed" but we're not in agreement with Him.

How is it that I say that we're not in agreement with Him? God has given us instructions in how to live a blessed life, but we are choosing death and cursing, instead of life and blessing. How many of you know that if I give you the recipe to make a cake and you follow that recipe to the letter that the cake will come out all right. But if you choose to add an extra sprinkle of salt and an extra egg, the cake is not going to taste like what the recipe said. Do you agree? It's just common sense.

Let's say you gave someone directions that tell him to go up to the light and turn right and then turn left. If the person goes to the light and turns left and then turns right how many people know that he will be lost? We have to learn to follow instructions, but we think that we are smarter than God. We say, "The Lord doesn't understand; He doesn't understand all the particulars surrounding my life so I'm going to help him out." The first thing we do is begin to make our own set of rules, our own righteousness and we go by those rules. Then we wonder why things aren't working for us. We look at God and say, "Why God? You understand my situation. You know." We won't even allow Him to correct us; we confess in prayer that He understands. We don't want to hear what He has to say because He might say something that's going to cause us to change our minds about what we're doing.

Try telling that to your boss. Try making your own rules with your boss. Try telling him, "Well I kind of slept in a little late, stayed out late you know." The boss won't understand that. In fact, your boss will tell you that if you continue doing this, you'll be out of a job. So if the boss is not going to put up with that, how do you think God will react? Like your boss, God will say, "It's your choice to make your own rules, but you won't see the blessing from it because you've chosen to follow another way." But if you're going to walk in the truth that the curse has been reversed, we've got the antidote. We've got a recipe. Amen?

Why Isn't It Working?

Now many of you are going to hear this, some are going to receive it, and others are going to disregard it altogether. It's natural, isn't it? Then they wonder three, four years down the road why they aren't walking in God's blessing. They will ask, "Why won't God smile on me?"

Isn't it sad how we've been taught to blame God when things don't go right for us? If we're not blessed, we think God is behind it—that He is mad at us because we're not doing everything right. People in the Old Testament could make this claim, but not us. Jesus came to resolve all issues with God so that He would no longer be angry with us. The Bible says that God is no longer holding our sins against us (Hebrews 8:12). God is for us, not against us. God is not our problem. He is the solution. It's not God who is refusing to bless. It's us who haven't applied God's system correctly. We have chosen to follow our own recipe and God would say, "Have you been following My recipe?"

Kingdom Building

The prophet Haggai was called to deal with some people who had been going through difficult times. They were trying to do everything in their power to make things good but kept falling short because they did not follow the recipe. So God called the prophet Haggai and told him to give those stiffnecked people the recipe again in hope that they would abide by it. We want the days of living paycheck to paycheck to be over. And so we need to know how to do this.

Thus speaketh the LORD of hosts, saying, This people say, The time is not come, the time that the LORD's house should be built. Then came the word of the LORD by Haggai the prophet, saying, Is it time for you, O ye, to dwell in your ceiled houses, and this house lie waste? Now therefore thus saith the LORD of hosts; Consider your ways. Ye have sown much, and bring in little; ye eat, but ye have not enough; ye drink, but ye are not filled with drink; ye clothe you, but there is none warm; and he that earneth wages earneth wages to put it into a bag with holes. [Haggai 1:2-6]

I want to establish something from the beginning. This is the Lord speaking, not Pastor Washington. He says, *This people say, The time is not come, the time that the LORD's house should be built.* In other words, the people were saying that they were not ready to build God's house. It wasn't time because they were presently building their own houses. Are you with me? How many of us are building our own houses? It seems that we do not do what God says because we are busy building our own houses.

Therefore we're wondering why we're still in such a position, because we're not focused on building His kingdom. We've placed building our own houses above building God's kingdom. He goes on to say, *Is it time for you, O ye, to dwell in your ceiled houses, and this house lie waste?* We've got selfishness within ourselves and we need to break free from it. God says, "Is this what you want? You want to live in your house while my house lies in waste?" What happens if a tornado comes and destroys your house? You're going to run to God's house to seek help. "God, can you help me? Can you help me, Lord? I lost my job, Father. Can you help me?" In times of trouble, you run to His house, but you

> **BENEFITS**
> **Your precious possessions will not wear out before their time. You will get proper usage out of your assets. (Malachi 3:11).**

don't want to help build it.

The opposite was true with King Solomon. According to the Bible, Solomon's primary focus was to build God's house first—to consecrate his resources and energies on establishing the blueprint handed down by his father David. In doing so, God blessed Solomon with a magnificent house.

What did God say? *Consider your ways.* When the Lord says, Consider your ways," he is talking about you... no one is exempt. We need to start looking at our ways. Amen? In other words God is saying, "I'm getting ready to give you an antidote—the recipe." God is going to start with you. He's not going to start with your boss; He's not going to start with your spouse; He's not going to start with this or that. He's going to start with you.

We are so quick to point the finger, aren't we? God is talking about you and me. He says, *Consider your ways. Ye have sown much, and bring in little; ye eat, but ye have not enough; ye drink, but ye are not filled with drink; ye clothe you, but there is none warm; and he that earneth wages earneth wages to put it into a bag with holes.* [Haggai 1:5-7]

The Lord breaks the people's lives down. He knew

that they had been sowing much but bringing in little. They had been feeding themselves, but there seemed not to be enough. They had clothes but were not warm, and whatever money they were earning was like they were putting it into a bag with holes.

God said, *Thus saith the Lord of hosts: Consider your ways.* God had been checking them out. You don't have enough; you are living paycheck to paycheck. This is happening because of your ways. Then God said:

Go up to the mountain, and bring wood, and build the house; and I will take pleasure in it, and I will be glorified, saith the LORD. Ye looked for much, and, lo, it came to little; and when ye brought it home, I did blow upon it. Why? saith the LORD of hosts. Because of mine house that is waste, and ye run every man unto his own house. Therefore the heaven over you is stayed from dew, and the earth is stayed from her fruit. And I called for a drought upon the land, and upon the mountains, and upon the corn, and upon the new wine, and upon the oil, and upon that which the ground bringeth forth, and upon men, and upon cattle, and upon all the labour of the hands. [Haggai 1:8-11]

Now what house is he talking about? His house.

God's kingdom—not a building, but a family of people. He said, *Go up to the mountain, and bring wood, and build the house; and I will take pleasure in it.* When God gets happy, watch out. When God's pleasure is flowing, things will change in your life. Doesn't the Bible say "that without faith it is impossible to please Him"? (Hebrews 11:6) God was calling them to seek Him first—to seek the building of His kingdom first with the promise that His pleasure would change things. It's just like when Jesus said, *Seek ye first the kingdom of God and his righteousness, and all these things shall be added unto you.* [Matthew 6:33]

If God gets happy, it's like turning a faucet wide open and His blessings will flow down. God said, *I will take pleasure in it.* Oh, if you want to please God, build His house first—His kingdom. The Bible says, *and I will be glorified, saith the Lord.*

He goes on to say; *Ye look for much, and lo, it came to little.* Their expectation was great; they were expecting a great windfall. You may have thought that this was the time, but then your expectation came to little and you were sour because you didn't get what you were expecting. When they brought it home, what did God do? He blew upon it. He said, *I did blow upon it. Consider your ways…*

God said, *I did blow upon it* and then someone asked the question, "Why? I worked all these weeks and hours, why did you blow on it? *"Because of mine house that is waste, and ye run every man unto his own house.* In other words they were more concerned about their houses, their situations, their businesses, and what they were doing than they were about God's house. God said, "If you build my house, I will take pleasure in it." We're talking about the curse being reversed, right?

Moreover, God is saying that He has set up a system—a recipe for success, and the first ingredient is to participate in building His kingdom. But if you don't put the right ingredient in first, then the rest will just blow away. This is a *system*—a spiritual law—that needs to be obeyed in order to get the right results. This law is like the law of electricity. The power company supplies the electricity to a building and it is flowing toward this building. However, if you don't use the correct wiring system, you will not get the correct results. It would be foolish to blame the power company for our refusal to obey the instructions. They are certainly not responsible.

In the same way, God is not responsible if you're not getting the intended results. God has set up a system; and in order to reap the benefits of this system, we must follow the instructions. Amen?

Because they didn't help build the house of God, He said, *Therefore the heaven over you is stayed from dew, and the earth is stayed from her fruit.* I like the way the Lord makes it personal: "the heaven over you". Others may be doing what they're supposed to be doing, but if YOU are not participating, then it's like you've turned off the faucet. Have you ever seen when it rains in one spot, and another spot there was no rain? One summer my wife and I were coming home, and this was during the time of drought in our area. All the grass was dying. As we turned into our neighborhood it started raining—pouring down, but once we turned onto our street, there was no rain.

What I'm saying today is that God said the heaven over us will not produce rain. In essence it will be closed. You could live right beside someone else and the heaven on that person can be open but the heaven upon you could be closed. Read what the scripture says: *Therefore the heaven over you is stayed from dew, and the earth is stayed from her fruit.* You know that fruit is a blessing and seeds cannot produce fruit without water. This is a natural law. God said that the earth held back from you; the heaven was shut up over you. Does it ever seem that wherever you walk things aren't working for you? We need to examine ourselves... *Consider your ways.*

God said, *And I called for a drought upon the land, and upon the mountains, and upon the corn, and upon the new wine, and upon the oil, and upon that which the ground bringeth forth, and upon men, and upon cattle, and upon all the labour of the hands.*

God says that because you aren't following His plan there are consequences. There is a cause and effect to everything. Because they had not built God's house first, the effects were that the earth would not produce fruit. *Their actions* had caused a drought upon the land. It wasn't that God cursed them. They chose which path to take and they had to suffer consequences.

It's much like the law of gravity. Gravity was created by God to be used for a good purpose, but when not used correctly, someone could get hurt. If a man jumps off a building, he will fall to the ground. God established this law to help us, right? Gravity keeps us grounded, and keeps our things from floating away. But, if not used properly, gravity can kill you. It's not

God who drags a person to the ground—it's the man's fault for not using it properly. This happened because they did not follow the directions of a spiritual law, and because they didn't, there were consequences.

The good news is that we can apply this law to our benefit by simply following the instructions God has given us. God has given us the truth that the curse has been reversed, but we have to walk in it. He has set before us life and death, blessing and cursing; and it is up to us to choose life—it's not up to God (Deuteronomy 30:19). God has established His system and in order to benefit from it, we must cooperate with His instructions.

The Wisdom of Tithing

Will a man rob God? Yet ye have robbed me. But ye say, Wherein have we robbed thee? In tithes and offerings. Ye are cursed with a curse: for ye have robbed me, even this whole nation. Bring ye all the tithes into the storehouse, that there may be meat in mine house, and prove me now herewith, saith the LORD of hosts, if I will not open you the windows of heaven, and pour you out a blessing, that there shall not be room enough to receive it. And I will rebuke the devourer for your sakes, and he shall not destroy the fruits of your ground; neither shall your vine cast her fruit before the time in the field, saith the LORD of hosts. And all nations shall call you blessed: for ye shall be a delightsome land, saith the LORD of hosts. [Malachi 3:8-12]

> **Did You Know?**
>
> <u>Great Men of God Who Paid Tithes</u>
>
> - Abraham (Gen. 14:20)
> - Jacob (Gen. 28:22)
> - Hezekiah (2 Chron. 31)
> - Nehemiah (Neh. 13)
> - David (1 Chron. 21:22-26)
> - Solomon (Pro. 3:9-10)

We've all read and heard the teachings about tithing from Malachi 3, and my point of interest is not to bring any fear upon you or to force you to do anything above what you want to do. My point of interest is to inform you and to give you wisdom that you might walk in the land of the living and that the blessing of the Lord might follow you.

The Bible says my people are destroyed for lack of knowledge (Hosea 4:6), and many people do not correctly teach us about finances. We all learn the law of receiving and I'm not minimizing the fact that you cannot give what you have never received. But there's a balance to this—and this balance comes in the form of giving. Jesus said, *Freely you have received, freely give.* [Matthew 10:8] There is always something you can give back in return. We will talk about sowing and reaping, the power of giving in a later chapter of this book.

The world says, "Get all you can, and *can* all you get," referring to the canning and storing of fruits and vegetables. This creates a selfish attitude with their mouth always open, but their hands closed. But Jesus said, *Give and it shall be given unto thee.* [Luke 6:38] God's system is completely different from the world. Because you have received freely, you should also give freely.

Will A Man Rob God?

The Bible asks this question: *Will a man rob God?* Many people have been taught that this verse represents a scenario of someone getting held up at gunpoint—that by not tithing we are in essence stealing God's money. I'd like to share a different perspective of this, one of which is not often presented.

Let's say that a friend wants to give you something—a brand new car, for example. But for whatever reason you refused to receive it. I know this sounds odd, but many people, because of pride, have problems with receiving freely because what they have has always been tied with performance or earnings.

You can witness this firsthand when people argue over who's paying for dinner at a restaurant. His friend would then try to convince him to receive this blessing by saying, "Don't rob me of this blessing."

Do you see what I'm talking about? Jesus said, *It is more blessed to give than to receive.* [Acts 20:35] Do you not think that God lives up to His own laws? Does God say, "Do as I say and not as I do?" No. It actually blesses God to give to you, but when you don't follow His system of opening up the windows of heaven, the flow is shut off. It's more accurate to say that by not tithing, we are tying God's hands behind His back. We are clogging up the pipe through which prosperity flows.

Partnering With God

The scriptures say that every good gift and every perfect gift comes from above (James 1:17) and God makes the sun to rise on the evil and the good; and sends rain on the just as well as the unjust (Matthew 5:45). So you will agree that God has blessed you, that God has sustained you and that you didn't do it with your own power. We learned in a previous chapter that God has given us the power to get wealth. So you have pleased God by receiving His blessing, but when you refuse to give back, it's as if you are robbing Him.

We can see this as a partnership. For example, God gives you $100 and establishes a partnership. Or, He opens the door to get you a job. Either way, because He has given you the power to get wealth, this money or job has come from God. Therefore, you and God are partners. You may not see it like that, but it doesn't matter how you see it. This is how God sees it. It's important for you to get in agreement with God—not the other way around.

> **Tithing Tips**
>
> The principle of tithing is the greatest investment in the world. It is also the greatest insurance policy one can have. (Malachi 3:11)

Since God established this partnership, when your check comes in, He asks that you do your part in giving the first portion of it back. God has done His part, and now He expects you, as a partner, to do yours. But you may say, "I can't give that. My bills are due today."

God says, "I thought that we were partners. Don't you trust Me? I got you this job and you said we were partners, but you won't trust Me enough to work the system I established?"

You know, if I wanted to learn how to effectively implement the assembly line system, I wouldn't ask someone who sold cars. I would ask the inventor of this system, Henry Ford. I wouldn't argue with him about this and that. I would trust that he knew what he was talking about since he was the one who created it.

So, why do we argue with God about the system He has created? Why don't we simply trust the Inventor so we can work the system effectively?

God is saying, "Did I not touch the man's heart to call you? Didn't I move mountains for you? Then why can't you share the dividends?"

We wonder why the boss calls and says, "We won't be needing your services anymore." Who will you run to then? You will say, "Oh Lord, the people said they don't need me. What am I going to do?"

God says, *Consider your ways.*

God's Grace and Mercy Are Free

Do you think that people are going to give you welfare because they want to? God started welfare in the Bible by leading us to feed the poor and help widows and orphans (Lev. 23:22; Lev. 19:9-10; Ex. 23:11; Deut. 24:19). It was a work welfare system intended to help people until they could find a job. Ruth was in this welfare system as a gleaner; and later, she became a reaper and owner of the same field from which she previously gleaned (Ruth 2-4).

The Bible says, *Let him that stole steal no more; but rather let him labor with hands the thing which is good, that he may have to give to him that needeth.* [Ephesians 4:28] God is saying that He wants you to work so you can give—not to live.

It was the mercy of God that established many things we have in this country. Did you know that the first schools were started by Christians? Did you know that the reformation of prisons and the system of rehabilitation were started by Christians? We know that the government runs these things now, but they were established out of God's mercy.

Most people don't have compassion for the homeless. They would let them be homeless and live on the street. Had it not been for the mercy of God there would be no food stamps. Had it not been for the mercy of God there would not be Medicaid. There would be no shelters. There would not be places to help you pay your bills when you're past due had it not been for the mercy of God. You think people are just kind? The Bible says that a man's heart is evil in all his ways (Jeremiah 17:9).

We have these things because of the mercy of God. He wants to be your senior partner. When God blesses you, He wants you to give. Without being inspired by God, no one is going to come by your house and give you $100.

So how have we robbed God? God says in tithes and offerings, you are cursed with a curse. Now most people think by this verse that God is cursing them. That's not what the Bible says. It says, "You are cursed with a curse" meaning that *you* have chosen death over life, and cursing over blessing by not participating in God's system. But because God has redeemed us from the curse, we can apply God's word to our life and be successful. God's blessing is given to us entirely by His grace—as a free gift. However, in order to have access to this grace, we must trust in what God's word says that gives us access. This is faith (Romans 5:2).

God said, *Bring ye all the tithes into the storehouse, that there may be meat in mine house,* Where did He say to bring them? Did He say to bring them down the street? No. He said to bring them to the storehouse. Like God's house in Haggai, the storehouse represents building His kingdom. He's talking about supporting the work of the ministry—the church.

Do not go down the street to give God's money away. Bring God's money to the storehouse. Once you place it in the storehouse, it's not your concern. Jesus had a treasurer that was stealing money. His name was Judas and the Bible calls him a thief (John 12:6) If some of you had been there in that day, you might have said, "I'm not going to sow into that ministry; they have a thief down there."

Yet this was Jesus, the Son of God, King of Kings, Lord of Lords, healing people, but we see that His treasurer was named Judas and he's stealing the money! You come to give God His money; you're not giving it to man. You have to see that you have a relationship with the Lord. You give this in the mighty name of Jesus. It is an act of faith and obedience that you give it because you trust God and want to live a blessed life—you are choosing blessing. Aren't you tired of living half way and barely getting by? You can stop it here by believing first that God has reversed the curse, and then trust in His plan for you to be blessed.

God told us to *Bring ye all the tithes into the storehouse, that there may be meat in mine house.* Meat can represent the meat of the word as in Hebrews 5:14 that will bring about mature Christians, but it can also represent general provision. Part of the church's mission is to help people that fall on hard times. If you're not paying your tithes how can the house be able? It's all part of God's financial plan.

God knows that money can be your greatest god. Jesus said, *No man can serve two masters. For either he will hate the one, and love the other; or else he will hold to the one, and despise the other. You cannot serve God and mammon* (money). [Matthew 6:24] He wants to be your God—your everything. The Bible says, *Honor the LORD with thy substance, and with the firstfruits of all thine increase.* [Proverbs 3:9]

God wants you to worship Him with your substance and worship Him with your mind. He wants you to worship Him, that He might take pleasure in your prosperity (Psalm 35:27). If God says He takes pleasure in your giving, His promises to take care of you are absolute.

Consider your ways.

Prove God's Word

The final part of this is the challenge God lays in front of us. The Bible says, *prove me now herewith, saith the LORD of hosts, if I will not open you the windows of heaven, and pour you out a blessing, that there shall not be room enough to receive it.* [Malachi 3:10]

God says, "Prove me." You've tried it your way; you've tried it momma's way; you've tried it everybody's way; so let's try God's way and see. God said, "Prove me, challenge me on this." Remember earlier we learned that the windows were closed; they were shut up. God says, "If I will not open you up the windows of heaven, and pour you out a blessing." The word "blessing" is a continuation—blessing—a constant flow.

But it doesn't stop there, God also said, *And I will rebuke the devourer for your sakes.* [Malachi 3:11] When someone tries to take advantage of you, when someone tries to get more than what they should get, God said you will have supernatural protection from the devourer for your sake. When you cooperate with God's system, you open the windows of heaven, and close the door to the devil. This is God's plan.

The Bible says, *Know ye not to whom ye yield yourselves servants to obey, his servants ye are to whom ye obey; whether of sin unto death, or obedience unto righteousness?* [Romans 6:16] When you refuse to cooperate with God's plan, you open the door wide to Satan and his death by virtue of this spiritual law. God is not unleashing the devil on you when you refuse to trust Him. Trusting in God's plan is part of being strong in the Lord and in the power of his might. The shield of faith is part of the whole armor of God that you may be able to stand against the wiles of the devil (Ephesians 6:10-16).

We have the best insurance policy a man can have. We have the best investment vessel a man can have. If you think that investing in the stock market is wise, you should try investing in God. But God said, *I will rebuke the devourer for your sake and he shall not destroy the fruits of your ground; neither shall your vine cast her fruit before the time in the field, saith the LORD of hosts. And all nations shall call you blessed: for ye shall be a delightsome land, saith the LORD of hosts.*

Do you *know* what that means? The crop you've sown through giving will be healthy and mature. Have you ever eaten a piece of fruit that wasn't completely ripe? It's usually sour. In the matter of grapes, the longer they stay on the vine, the sweeter they get. God is saying that your harvest will be complete—mature, not immature.

God is also speaking of time. When you invest money in a 6-month CD, it takes six months to "mature." What happens if you withdraw it before the maturity date? It costs you, right? There's a penalty. This is what God means when He says, "Your vine will not cast her fruit before its time; your clothes will not wear out before they should; your vehicle will not constantly break down." We'll talk more about this in the chapter "Sowing and Reaping".

God knows how to sustain your fruit. This is the promise God gives you. Your vine will last longer even though someone tries to get over on you.

Let God's word work for you. You see the promises right here. You're reading it for yourself. God is faithful to His word. He said, "Prove me." He goes on to say, "And all nations shall call you blessed." You can get no greater person to validate you than God who said that all nations shall call you blessed.

Do people around you call you "blessed"?

When you trust God's word, He is faithful to live up to His word.

chapter 5

Place a Demand on Heaven

Thus saith the LORD, the Holy One of Israel, and his Maker, Ask me of things to come concerning my sons, and concerning the work of my hands command ye me.

Just as we walk in the fact that the curse has been reversed, we can also apply the principles of tithing in reverse. Similar to the equation $2 + 3 = 5$, we know that $3 + 2$ also equals 5. While we reversed the order of the numbers, the results are still the same. The law of the firstfruits tells us to *Honour the LORD with thy substance, and with the firstfruits of all thine increase.* [Proverbs 3:9] But must we wait for the increase to come to apply the principles and benefits of tithing? Since the laws of tithing apply also in reverse order, we can place a demand upon God's promise to give increase to a seed sown in faith even before we receive the increase.

My mother-in-law Dianne was able to benefit from this principle and I want to share this with you so you too can benefit. God spoke through the prophet Isaiah and said, *Thus saith the LORD, the Holy One of Israel... concerning the work of my hands command ye me.* [Isaiah 45:11]

Dianne was in a precarious position and needed finances quickly. Applying this principle, Dianne decided to pay her tithes in advance by sowing $1,000 into the kingdom of God, standing upon God's promise that He would provide the $10,000 increase from which the tithe came. I was so impressed by her faith and willingness to give, that my wife and I agreed with her in prayer. While praying, the Lord gave me revelation of the truth of reversing this principle and still receiving the benefits. Dianne's faith was that God would supply a $10,000 increase, and she paid the $1,000 tithe on it in advance. Now this is faith in action.

During the prayer, we asked God to honor the advance payment and respond with a $10,000 increase. The principle prevailed and God responded with $10,000, and shortly thereafter, the Lord supplied an additional $10,000 to her. It was if God was saying, "My reputation is on the line. You have crossed the plane of my circle, knocked the stick off my shoulder, and I have responded with a double portion." I recalled His promise, *that there shall not be room enough to receive it.* [Malachi 3:10]

Of course in response to the double portion increase by God, Dianne sowed an additional $1,000.

This reminded me of two incidents in the Old Testament where someone exercised faith in God's promises and the person received great blessings from God. The first example is Isaac where he obeyed God's instructions to dwell in the land of Gerar during a famine and because of his faith and obedience, he received a hundredfold harvest from what he sowed in the land. We read the account of this in Genesis 26:1-6; 12-14

And there was a famine in the land, beside the first famine that was in the days of Abraham. And Isaac went unto Abimelech king of the Philistines unto Gerar. And the LORD appeared unto him, and said, Go not down into Egypt; dwell in the land which I shall tell thee of: Sojourn in this land, and I will be with thee, and will bless thee; for unto thee, and unto thy seed, I will give all these countries, and I will perform the oath which I sware unto Abraham thy father; And I will make thy seed to multiply as the stars of heaven, and will give unto thy seed all these countries; and in thy seed shall all the nations of the earth be blessed; Because that Abraham obeyed my voice, and kept my charge, my commandments, my statutes, and my laws. And Isaac dwelt in Gerar:

...Then Isaac sowed in that land, and received in the same year an hundredfold: and the LORD blessed him. And the man waxed great, and went forward, and grew until he became very great: For he had possession of flocks, and possession of herds, and great store of servants: and the Philistines envied him.

We see here that Isaac sowed in the land that had been struck with a famine, but yet because of his faith in God's word, he received a hundredfold return, which caused others to see him as great and envy him. Who in his right mind would plant seeds in the middle of a famine? Famine means a severe shortage of food resulting in a widespread hunger. In most cases, famine comes about through drought—a period of dry weather when there is not enough rain for the successful growing of crops. For example, several years ago we watched the many images flash across our televisions

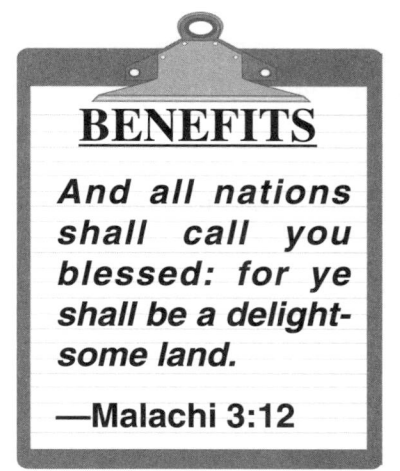

> **BENEFITS**
>
> *And all nations shall call you blessed: for ye shall be a delightsome land.*
>
> —Malachi 3:12

of Ethiopia going through a famine. The land was dry and there was no vegetation.

Isaac acted on faith in God's word. The ground was dry and the sky was without rain, but yet he planted his seed anyway. In that he sowed his seed in faith as a response to God's word, he received a hundredfold return.

Perhaps you find yourself in a similar position. Don't eat the seed—sow it! Place a demand on Heaven to respond to your giving (Genesis 26:12).

Another example occurred when Solomon made an offering to the Lord and reaped perhaps the greatest blessings anyone in the Old Testament had ever received.

And Solomon loved the LORD, walking in the statutes of David his father: only he sacrificed and burnt incense in high places. And the king went to Gibeon to sacrifice there; for that was the great high place: a thousand burnt offerings did Solomon offer upon that altar. In Gibeon the LORD appeared to Solomon in a dream by night: and God said, Ask what I shall give thee. And Solomon said, Thou hast showed unto thy servant David my father great mercy, according as he walked before thee in truth, and in righteousness, and in uprightness of heart with thee; and thou hast kept for him this great kindness, that thou hast given him a son to sit on his throne, as it is this day. And now, O LORD my God, thou hast made thy servant king instead of David my father: and I am but a little child: I know not how to go out or come in. And thy servant is in the midst of thy people which thou hast chosen, a great people, that cannot be numbered nor counted for multitude. Give therefore thy servant an understanding heart to judge thy people, that I may discern between good and bad: for who is able to judge this thy so great a people?

And the speech pleased the Lord, that Solomon had asked this thing. And God said unto him, Because thou hast asked this thing, and hast not asked for thyself long life; neither hast asked riches for thyself, nor hast asked the life of thine enemies; but hast asked for thyself understanding to discern judgment; Behold, I have done according to thy words: lo, I have given thee a wise and an understanding heart; so that there was none like thee before thee, neither after thee shall any arise like unto thee. And I have also given thee that which thou hast not asked, both riches, and honour: so that there shall not be any among the kings like unto thee all thy days. And if thou wilt walk in my ways, to keep my statutes and my commandments, as thy father David did walk, then I will lengthen thy days. [1 Kings 3:3-14]

We see that Solomon made a similar offering as Dianne did—a thousand burnt offerings vs. $1,000—and this prompted the Lord's blessing to come in a great measure: *God said, Ask what I shall give thee.* Then when Solomon asked for wisdom instead of riches or long life, God was so pleased that not only did He give the king wisdom to rule the people of Israel, but also riches and honor that would exceed any of the kings in his days. Do you see the power of taking the principles of God's word and making them active in your life?

> **Tithing Tips**
>
> God gives seed to the sower and bread to the eater. If He can get it **through** you, He will get it **to** you.

Finally, the account of the widow's mite as recorded in Mark 12:41-44 is a great example of placing a demand upon Heaven in dire circumstances. *And Jesus sat over against the treasury, and beheld how the people cast money into the treasury: and many that were rich cast in much. And there came a certain poor widow, and she threw in two mites, which make a farthing. And he called unto him his disciples, and saith unto them, Verily I say unto you, That this poor widow hath cast more in, than all they which have cast into the treasury: For all they did cast in of their abundance; but she of her want did cast in all that she had, even all her living.*

The fact that Jesus noted her condition (widow, alone, poor, all she had) we believe He had compassion to fulfill her needs and desires that day. Heaven responded to the faith that caused the seed to be sown by her, and I believe it will respond likewise to you.

Purpose Your Seed!

In the beginning of 2007, my mother Juliette purposed a seed of $30,000 toward the building of Whole Man Ministries. The seed she purposed was sown specifically to purchase the building that houses our church and ministry headquarters.

The Bible teaches that a seed brings forth fruit after its own kind (Genesis 1:11). Therefore, if you want to grow apples, you must plant apple seeds and so on. The Bible says, *for whatsoever a man soweth, that shall he also reap.* [Galatians 6:7] This principle can also be applied to giving as the apostle Paul taught in 2 Corinthians 9:10, *Now he that ministereth seed to the sower both minister bread for your food, and multiply your seed sown, and increase the fruits of your righteousness.*

For example, we see that God planted a seed (a word) in Genesis 3:15; and then the Holy Spirit planted this seed into Mary's womb, which eventually led to the birth of Jesus and the redemption of mankind (Luke 1:30-33). Of course we know the famous passage from John 3:16, *For God so loved the world, that <u>he gave</u> his only begotten Son, that whosoever believeth in him should not perish, but have everlasting life.*

Jesus expands on this principle when He likens His own death as a seed sown in order to produce much fruit. *Verily, verily, I say unto you, Except a corn of wheat fall into the ground and die, it abideth alone: but if it die, it bringeth forth much fruit.* [John 12:24] The "fruit" the Lord is referring to is us as the Scripture calls Jesus the *firstborn among many brethren* (Romans 8:29) and also the firstfruits (1 Corinthians 15:20-23).

Taking these principles then, we can see that in order to get a specific need fulfilled (harvest) you must plant a seed of its own kind. We have a great example of this in the Old Testament when the prophet

Elijah was sent to a widow woman in Zarephath.

And the word of the LORD came unto him, saying, Arise, get thee to Zarephath, which belongeth to Zidon, and dwell there: behold, I have commanded a widow woman there to sustain thee. So he arose and went to Zarephath. And when he came to the gate of the city, behold, the widow woman was there gathering of sticks: and he called to her, and said, Fetch me, I pray thee, a little water in a vessel, that I may drink. And as she was going to fetch it, he called to her, and said, Bring me, I pray thee, a morsel of bread in thine hand.

And she said, As the LORD thy God liveth, I have not a cake, but an handful of meal in a barrel, and a little oil in a cruse: and, behold, I am gathering two sticks, that I may go in and dress it for me and my son, that we may eat it, and die.

And Elijah said unto her, Fear not; go and do as thou hast said: but make me thereof a little cake first, and bring it unto me, and after make for thee and for thy son. For thus saith the LORD God of Israel, The

> **Did You Know?**
>
> *He which soweth sparingly shall reap also sparingly; and he which soweth bountifully shall reap also bountifully.*
>
> —2 Corinthians 9:6

barrel of meal shall not waste, neither shall the cruse of oil fail, until the day that the LORD sendeth rain upon the earth.

And she went and did according to the saying of Elijah: and she, and he, and her house, did eat many days. And the barrel of meal wasted not, neither did the cruse of oil fail, according to the word of the LORD, which he spake by Elijah. [1 Kings 17:8-16]

This woman was desperate. She had enough to make just one cake for her and her son and then they would starve and die. However, at the direction of the man of God, and instead of eating her seed, she chose to plant it, which produced an abundant supply of food for her and her family. The seed she planted produced after its own kind!

You have the authority to assign a specific purpose for your seed. In essence, this means that you can plant a seed toward a goal or purpose. For example, if you're in debt, plant seeds that will produce freedom from debt. This is not contrary to the nature of a seed producing after its own kind. You cannot take orange seeds and "claim" them to be apple seeds. Rather this is a biblical principle of giving that allows you to plant something that inherently has no seed in itself (like money) and use it as a seed for a specific purpose.

King David used this principle for the purpose of building God's temple. Because of David's sins, the people of Israel were being destroyed, and David sought means to stay the destruction by seeking the LORD. The LORD sent the prophet Gad to David who told him to build an altar of the LORD in the threshingfloor of Araunah the Jebusite, of which David purchased for the sum of 600 shekels of gold and 50 shekels of silver (2 Samuel 24:22-25; 1 Chronicles 21:22-26).

The effects of this offering were twofold: the plague was stayed; and the seed to build the temple was planted, only to be reaped years later. The exact same place where David built the altar of the LORD is where Solomon began building God's temple (2 Chronicles 3:1). This passage says, *Then Solomon began to build the house of the LORD at Jerusalem in mount Moriah, where the LORD appeared unto David his father, in the place that David had prepared in the threshingfloor of Ornan the Jebusite.* Ironically, Mt. Moriah is the same place where God led Abraham to sacrifice his son Isaac (Genesis 22:2).

Just as David did, my mother planted a seed that resulted in the building of our church and ministry headquarters. Therefore, as the saying goes, "If you have a need, plant a seed." Assign a purpose for what you give in faith that it will produce fruit after its own kind.

The Law of Supply and Demand

The world's view of enconomics teaches that if there is a demand, supply normally follows. However, in God's kingdom and because of His foreknowledge, God has already provided the supply before we have a need. Jesus said, *Be not ye therefore like unto them: for your Father knoweth what things ye have need of, before ye ask him.* [Matthew 6:8]

The Bible teaches that through Jesus, God *hath blessed us with all spiritual blessings in heavenly places in Christ.* [Ephesians 1:3] and that all things pertaining to life and godliness have been given to us through the knowledge of God (2 Peter 1:3).

In today's world, advertisers put enormous pressure on a consumer to respond by purchasing (more often than not) what they *want* instead of what they *need*. In a similar way, we can place a demand upon the promises of God that always say, "Yes and Amen to the glory of God by us..." (2 Corinthians 1:20) when we remember and act upon God's word.

The Lord said the following things:

Prove me now herewith, saith the LORD of hosts, if I will not open you the windows of heaven, and pour you out a blessing, that there shall not be room enough to receive it. [Malachi 3:10]

Put me in remembrance: let us plead together: declare thou, that you mayest be justified. [Isaiah 43:26]

Thou shalt also decree a thing, and it shall be established unto thee: and the light shall shine down upon thy ways. [Job 22:28]

If you remember the Lord Jesus' temptation in the wilderness, His response was always, "It is written" indicating that He was acting upon the word of God that released the power and authority to resist temptation.

So then, when we find a promise of God and, in faith, place a demand upon God's word, we are activating the power and authority of God to be released to accomplish whatever the word promises.

And when we make an offering, we are placing a demand upon the promises of God that say, I will *open you the windows of heaven, and pour you out a blessing, that there shall not be room enough to receive it.* Our declaration of faith does not remind God of His own word as if He suffered from memory loss; nor does it cause God to *move on your behalf*, because God has already moved through Jesus, and given us all things that pertain to life and godliness (2 Peter 1:3). Rather, faith opens the door by which God's promises can be accessed and released into your life (Romans 5:2).

By placing a demand upon Heaven, you have released the power and authority of God's word to respond on your behalf.

From Rags to Riches: The Story of Jacob

chapter 6

And the man increased exceedingly, and had much cattle, and maidservants, and menservants, and camels, and asses. [Genesis 30:43]

An investment in God's kingdom can reap a hundredfold return, not only in money, but spiritually, emotionally, physically, and in health. Jacob made an investment; he took out an insurance claim with God. He was a poor man without family, money, goals, and vision until he trusted in God to give him a breakthrough.

Jacob was suffering the most difficult time of his life. In fear of the vengeful hand of his brother Esau, he had fled his home at the request of his mother and father. Alone, afraid, and alienated, Jacob turned to God in desperation and unlocked the door of prosperity through a spiritual law that exists today—the tithe.

We know that Jacob was a deceiver who tricked his brother to give him his birthright in exchange for a morsel of food. He'd also deceived his own father, taking advantage of his blindness to obtain his brother's blessing. Fleeing from the wrath of his brother, Jacob happened upon a place and had an encounter with God that would change his life forever. God revealed Himself to Jacob in a dream where he saw a ladder that reached from earth to heaven with angels ascending and descending on it.

> **Tithing Tips**
>
> Give unto Caesar what is Caesar's; and unto God what is God's. So many have given Caesar his portion, but very few give God his portion.

And, behold, the LORD stood above it, and said, I am the LORD God of Abraham thy father, and the God of Isaac: the land whereon thou liest, to thee will I give it, and to thy seed; And thy seed shall be as the dust of the earth, and thou shalt spread abroad to the west, and to the east, and to the north, and to the south: and in thee and in thy seed shall all the families of the earth be blessed. And, behold, I am with thee, and will keep thee in all places whither thou goest, and will bring thee again into this land; for I will not leave thee, until I have done that which I have spoken to thee of.

And Jacob awaked out of his sleep, and he said, Surely the LORD is in this place; and I knew it not. And he was afraid, and said, How dreadful is this place! this is none other but the house of God, and this is the gate of heaven. And Jacob rose up early in the morning, and took the stone that he had put for his pillows, and set it up for a pillar, and poured oil upon the top of it. And he called the name of that place Bethel: but the name of that city was called Luz at the first. And Jacob vowed a vow, saying, If God will be with me, and will keep me in this way that I go, and will give me bread to eat, and raiment to put on, So that I come again to my father's house in peace; then shall the LORD be my God: And this stone, which I have set for a pillar, shall be God's house: and of all that thou shalt give me I will surely give the tenth unto thee. [Genesis 28:14-22]

> **BENEFITS**
>
> *My God shall supply all your need according to his riches in glory by Christ Jesus.*
>
> —Philippians 4:19

When Jacob spoke the words of his vow, he put into motion a spiritual law that unlocked the windows of heaven. Let us note the final words from Jacob in this passage: *and of all that thou shalt give me I will surely give the tenth unto thee.*

Why would he make such a statement? Perhaps it was because he learned the principles of tithing from his father Isaac, who had learned it from his father Abraham. Abraham, the father of faith, completely understood the power of honoring God with the tithe. God had led Abraham from the land where his father Terah had served other gods (Joshua 24:2) to where he would serve the one true God. It was evident by his faith that he appreciated the blessings of God.

The account of Abraham paying tithes (Genesis 14:20-23) is the first reference to the firstfruits being a certain percentage. The Hebrew word •âśar is translated tithe or tenth, referring to the portion God has called holy and reserved for Himself. In response to being blessed by God through His high priest Melchisidec, Abraham offered the tenth of what belonged to him to not only honor God, but to demonstrate his trust that God was the source of all his wealth.

As a result of Abraham's faithfulness, God declared his confidence that the patriarch would pass along the wisdom of the firstfruits to his children and to his children's children. The Lord said, *For I know him, that he will command his children and his household after him, and they shall keep the way of the LORD, to do justice and judgment; that the LORD may bring upon Abraham that which he hath spoken of him.* [Genesis 18:19]

Knowing that Abraham taught this principle to his son Isaac, and in turn to Jacob, we see that in a dream, God gives Jacob a vision of the benefits of honoring God with the firstfruits. The ladder that extended from earth to heaven with angels ascending and descending was no coincidence, but a picture of the flow of God's power that is released by faith. **Paying the tithe, then, was a work of faith**, and continues to be a work of faith through our obedience toward God.

During this time in Jacob's life, he had no wife, no children, no cattle, no money. All he had was a staff and a promise from his father and from God. That was enough. We see that after twenty-one years, Jacob returned to his home with two wives, twelve sons, several thousand donkeys, sheep, goats, and cattle. How did this happen in such a short time? It was God's favor upon him that was released by faith and obedience in honoring God with the firstfruits. Jacob trusted God and kept his promise. God in turn, kept His word.

Jacob even made the confession of God's favor upon his own life to his father-in-law Laban. *And he said unto him, Thou knowest how I have served thee, and how thy cattle was with me. For it was little which thou hadst before I came, and it is now increased unto a multitude; and the LORD hath blessed thee since my coming: and now when shall I provide for mine own house also?* [Genesis 30:29-30]

Laban too acknowledged that he had been blessed through his association with Jacob by saying, *For I have learned by experience that the LORD hath blessed me for thy sake.* [Genesis 30:27]. This confession lends credence to the assertion that we can be blessed by association and also cursed by association.

God gives us a picture of Jacob's prosperity. He shows us first hand how Jacob went from rags to riches. This is a great example of how being obedient to God brings about change in a person's life and circumstances. It doesn't matter what level of business you're associated with; God will multiply it. Jacob was a farmer and because he was faithful, the Bible says, *And the man increased exceedingly, and had much cattle, and maidservants, and menservants, and camels, and asses.* [Genesis 30:43]

As God caused Jacob to increase in what he set his hand to, He will do the same for you, provided you trust in His ways. Paying tithes does not contradict the revelation of God's grace, just as works of faith do not make God move on your behalf. Rather, actions produced by faith unlocks the door to grant you access to all of God's grace. The Bible says, *Therefore being justified by faith, we have peace with God through our Lord Jesus Christ: By whom also we have access by faith into this grace wherein we stand, and rejoice in hope of the glory of God.* [Romans 5:1-2]

> **Did You Know?**
>
> <u>Five Purposes of Tithes</u>
>
> - **For priests**
> - **For the poor**
> - **To supply God's house (the church)**
> - **To honor God**
> - **Belongs to God**

The Bible says that the power of tithing unlocks the windows of Heaven (Malachi 3:10). Many of you find yourselves in debt to your necks, and find it difficult to even pay your bills, let alone pay the tithe. Even as you read this book, many of you are faced with foreclosures on your homes, past due notes on vehicles, mounting child care costs, doctor, light, and telephone bills and more.

The question you may be asking is, "How can I afford to devote 10% of my salary when I can barely pay my bills now?"

My answer is: How can you afford not to pay your tithes when it is the greatest protection plan, a greater assurance any insurance can provide. "Invest in Kingdom Building!" The practice of contributing 10% of your income to the building of God's kingdom is the greatest investment you can make. With God as CEO and also chief financial officer (CFO), you have the most effective economic system ever created, causing the world's system to pale in comparison. The world's system is focused on *addition*, while God's system guarantees *multiplication* when you invest in His kingdom. Once you begin trusting God in your finances, He guarantees that you will see change in your situation. God stands ready and willing to back His plan with these words, "Prove me!"

If I will not open you the windows of heaven, and pour you out a blessing, that there shall not be room enough to receive it. [Malachi 3:10]

Do what Jacob did. Trust God and see if His ways will cause you to have your own "Rags to Riches" story.

Sowing and Reaping

chapter 7

Be not deceived: God is not mocked: for whatsoever a man soweth, that shall he also reap. For he that soweth to his flesh shall of the flesh reap corruption; but he that soweth to the Spirit shall of the Spirit reap life everlasting. [Galatians 6:7-8]

First of all, I want to establish that I believe the Bible teaches that there is a difference between giving and tithing. Although they are compatible at times, there is a difference in application. The rule that governs giving is love. The Bible teaches that in order for the gift to be profitable, the giver must be motivated by love (1 Corinthians 13:1-3). Giving and the tithe are both governed by love. For the tithe, the love is for God; while in giving, the love is for people. The difference, however, is that the tithe is a heavenly obligation toward the building of God's kingdom while giving is retained in the will of the giver.

There is a spiritual law of giving. It's called the law of sowing and reaping. Whatever we sow we will reap, whether in the flesh or in the spirit.

In other words, God is holding us accountable. Whatever seeds we sow, let them be good seeds, so we can reap a plentiful and bountiful harvest.

In order to understand the spiritual law of giving, we need only look to the greatest giver. Who is that? God is the greatest giver who sought to empty heaven and give all that He had for the salvation of mankind.

Can you imagine when God looked around heaven and said, "What can I give to redeem man?" And He looked and saw that there was no greater thing of value than His only begotten Son. The palace wasn't enough. The throne wasn't enough. God said, "I'm going to give all I have for mankind. I will give of Myself."

If you take God's word and make it applicable to your life, it will produce change for the good. You will see that God's power will become active in your life, behind the scenes, if you make His word applicable. Now that means living it, acting upon the word. The Bible says, *Even so faith, if it hath not works is dead, being alone.* [James 2:17]

We're going to learn about giving. Giving happens to be part of God's financial plan. God has a financial plan for all of us, and His plan has in it giving, tithing, investing and so on, and in this chapter we are going to talk about giving. The gift of giving, sowing and reaping is one of God's spiritual laws.

Jesus said, "For God so loved the world that he gave..." What did He do? He gave. Giving has to come out of love. Are you with me? The motive behind giving has to be love. The Bible says that God so LOVED the world that He GAVE, and the same is true in a marriage. Our giving of ourselves has to come as a result of our love toward one another. Here God sees the world that He had created and He loved it, so He ultimately gave Himself.

The Bible says, *For God so loved the world that he gave his only begotten Son, that whosoever believeth in him should not perish, but have everlasting life.* [John 3:16]

Who is "whosoever"? That's you and me. That's everyone who believes in Him shall not perish but have everlasting life. God's purpose of giving is to give you a better life. Your purpose when you give to someone is to give them a better life, or a better opportunity at life.

God's gift came out of love. The motive behind the gift is love. He goes on and says that God gave not His gift to the world to condemn it, but through His gift the world might be saved. What the Lord is letting us know that when we give to others, it is out of love and not to condemn the recipient of the gift. Now we've all been guilty of that. We've given to someone and with the gift came a lecture, pointing the finger with a stern look of condemnation. I'm not saying that a gift shouldn't come with responsibility. Most gifts come with instructions. Even when God gave Christ, He gave us instructions. He was saying there is a responsibility for this gift that I'm giving you. We should give in order to help someone that couldn't otherwise get what they need. As with all blessings, there are responsibilities.

God said that He didn't send His son to condemn you. Therefore, the gift that we give is not to condemn the recipient. It is out of love that we give it, although with instructions. *For God sent not His son into the world to condemn the world but that the world through Him might be saved.* So that the world might be saved, God gave all He had for the salvation of mankind.

The Scripture says that *you were bought with a price* (1 Corinthians 6:20). It cost God to engraft us into the olive branch; and it cost Him blood, sweat and tears. In essence, God gave Himself. There's a story about an Native American that was sitting on the horse when he met a pastor. The pastor shared the gospel with him and said, "'God so loved the world that He gave His only begotten Son, that whosoever believes in Him should not perish, but have everlasting life.' The Indian rode down on his horse and said, 'Me Indian, give tomahawk.' He rode back up to the hill and the pastor repeated the words of Jesus. The Indian rode back down, and said, 'Me Indian give chief hat.' Once again, the preacher proclaimed God's word. The Indian rode back down and said, 'Me Indian give horse.' He went back. For the last time the preacher looked at the crowd and he proclaimed at the top of his voice, 'God so loved the world that He gave His only begotten Son that whosoever shall believe in Him shall not perish but have everlasting life.' The Indian came down to the altar, looked up at the pastor and said, 'Me Indian give self. I give you my self.' That's what God wants. The most precious gift that you have is yourself. God gave Himself that we might have eternal life."

I started with the passage

> **BENEFITS**
>
> *The curse of the LORD is in the house of the wicked: but he blesseth the habitation of the just.*
> **—Proverbs 3:33**

from John because I wanted to convey to you the importance of giving. God has given us an example how He wants us to give. In giving, Jesus said that what you give shall be given unto you again, pressed down and shaken together and running over, that men shall give unto your bosom (Luke 6:38). Give and it shall be given unto you. What a man sows, that shall he reap. That's a spiritual law that is eternal. Give and it shall be given unto you.

Can God put something in your hand if it's closed? It's impossible to put something in a hand that is closed. The hand of giving is open; and because it remains open, the giving hand is able also to receive. I had a friend who was always giving. He would almost give you the last thing that he had, but he never went lacking. He was applying the biblical principles of sowing and reaping. I didn't understand it until I became a Christian. He would always give and it seemed like he was doing less and had more, while I was doing more, but had less. He was giving and God was blessing him.

I have learned, in all relationships, that you have to give. You have to go beyond yourself. You have to step outside of the box. Things that are important to you may not be important to your spouse. So in order for your spouse to understand what is important to you, you've got to understand what's important to them. You want your sweetie to sit down and watch a basketball game with you every now and then? Then you find out what she likes to do, and be a part of it. You give and then it's given back to you. That's what giving is all about.

But this I say, He which soweth sparingly shall reap also sparingly; and he which soweth bountifully shall reap also bountifully. Every man according as he purposeth in his heart, so let him give; not grudgingly, or of necessity: for God loveth a cheerful giver. And God is able to make all grace abound toward you; that ye, always having all sufficiency in all things, may abound to every good work: (As it is written, He hath dispersed abroad; he hath given to the poor: his righteousness remaineth for ever. Now he that ministereth seed to the sower both minister bread for your food, and multiply your seed sown, and increase the fruits of your righteousness;) Being enriched in every thing to all bountifulness, which causeth through us thanksgiving to God. For the administration of this service not only supplieth the want of the saints, but is abundant also by many thanksgivings unto God; Whiles by the experiment of this ministration they glorify God for your professed subjection unto the gospel of Christ, and for your liberal distri-

bution unto them, and unto all men. [2 Corinthians 9:6-13]

Don't expect to receive a big harvest when you go to the field to plant corn but you only sow ten corn seeds. The scripture tells us if you sow sparingly you're going to reap sparingly. It is a spiritual law. But nevertheless whatever you sow you will reap. Now my definition of "sparingly" may be completely different than yours. You need to understand that. If I have ten dollars to my name and I give five, it may be more than a person who has a $100,000 and sows $10,000, because our situations are completely different. Wherein he sowed 10% of what he had, I sowed 50%. Which of the two sowed sparingly? God doesn't look at the amount, but the percentage of what you have.

We can see this in the account of the widow woman who offered two mites unto the Lord. Jesus testified that she had given more than anyone else because the others had given out of their abundance, but she had given all she had (Luke 21:1-4). His judgment was based upon her financial condition.

God said that whatever you sow, you're going to reap. If it's a little, than you're going to reap a little. If it's a lot, then you're going to reap a lot, provided it is done with the right motive. Therefore, the most important thing is that you open your hand and give. Let the Lord use you. The Bible says, *Every man according as he purposeth in his heart, so let him give; not grudgingly, or of necessity: for God loveth a cheerful giver.*

The word of God says that a giver has power over what he has. In other words, it's his choice to give or not to give. A person should give as he purposes in his own heart, not as an obligation or of necessity, because obligation and necessity remove love from the gift. You don't pay your bills because you love your creditors. You pay them because it's an obligation—because you need to keep your lights on. Therefore, because I say that the giver has no obligation to give, am I saying that it's not sin if you don't give? What is sin? It's falling short of God's standard, right? If God is the greatest giver of all, we should follow His example by giving generously out of love from the heart. Therefore, it's not a matter of sin or of the law. It's a matter of what's in your heart. Do you see the difference?

We see an example of this in the Bible with Ananias and Sapphira (Acts 5). The couple had promised to give a certain amount on the sale of property to the church. They were not obligated to give, but it was impressed upon their hearts to give—a gift inspired by love and need. However, after selling their property, they privately changed their minds and decided to give less than what they had promised.

But a certain man named Ananias, with Sapphira his wife, sold a possession, And kept back part of the price, his wife also being privy to it, and brought a certain part, and laid it at the apostles' feet. But Peter said, Ananias, why hath Satan filled thine heart to lie to the Holy Ghost, and to keep back part of the price of the land? Whiles it remained, was it not thine own? and after it was sold, was it not in thine own power? why hast thou conceived this thing in thine heart? thou hast not lied unto men, but unto God. [Acts 5:1-4]

The Bible says that Ananias and Sapphira had the right to give whatever they desired—whether less or more, it was within their power. However, they went about this the wrong way. Instead of coming to Peter privately and communicating their change of heart—a desire to give a different amount than promised, they chose to lie to God about the selling price of the land.

Peter made it perfectly clear that it was within their power to give whatever they had chosen, but their fault was lying about it—not just to Peter, but more importantly they lied to God. This account explains the difference between the spiritual law of giving versus the spiritual law of tithing. Both are done through faith; both are sown from the heart through love; both come with an expectation from God's word; and both work toward a common good—for God's kingdom and purpose.

While giving remains in the power of the giver to give or not to give, with the primary motive being love, tithing is sown in response to God's demand, an act of obedience and faith.

> **Tithing Tips**
> *The first of the firstfruits of thy land thou shalt bring into the house of the LORD thy God.*
> —Exodus 23:19

God loves a cheerful giver; and He says, "Don't give grudgingly." In other words if you want to help someone, do it. But if you do it grudgingly, it will not profit you. The motive behind your gift is more important than the gift. It will profit whomever you give to, but will not profit you. The Bible says, *And though I bestow all my goods to feed the poor, and though I give my body to be burned, and have not charity, it profiteth me nothing.*

Giving won't profit you if it's going to be a necessity. In other words, if someone is pressuring you to give, and you give out of pressure, it may not profit you. God says to give with a purpose in your heart to give. Because God is a giver, He is always encouraging you to follow Him in giving to others. Remember what I taught earlier, that God has blessed you so that you will be a blessing to others. He has given you the power to get wealth so that you may represent His giving heart here in this world. I know a prominent pastor whose license plate reads: LIV 2 GIV. I later learned that this pastor is truly a giver in more ways than one.

You also should not give in order to receive honor from people. Jesus said, *Take heed that ye do not your alms before men, to be seen of them: otherwise ye have no reward of your Father which is in heaven. Therefore when thou doest thine alms, do not sound a trumpet before thee, as the hypocrites do in the synagogues and in the streets, that they may have glory of men. Verily I say unto you, They have their reward.* [Matthew 6:1-2]

Jesus called people who gave in order to get praise and honor from man "hypocrites" and their reward was whatever credit or praise they got from man.

Occasionally in the law of giving, the Lord will impress upon your heart to give a certain amount. It behooves all of us to yield to the tugging of our hearts by God.

Let Every Man Be Persuaded

At the same time, let me remind you of a passage of Scripture that needs to be considered in light of this. The apostle Paul wrote, *Who art thou that judgest another man's servant? To his own master he standeth or falleth. Yea, he shall be holden up: for God is able to make him stand. One man esteemeth one day above another: another man esteemeth every day alike. Let every man be fully persuaded in his own mind. He that regardeth the day, regardeth it unto the Lord; and he that regardeth not the day, to the Lord he doth not regard it. He that eateth, eateth to the Lord, for he giveth thanks; and he that eateth not, to the Lord he eateth not, and giveth God thanks. For none of us liveth to himself, and no man dieth to himself. For whether we live, we live unto the Lord; and whether we die, we die unto the Lord: whether we live therefore, or die, we are the Lord's. For to this end Christ both died, and rose, and revived, that he might be Lord both of the dead and living.* [Romans 14:4-10]

Here Paul was dealing with matters of Old Testament traditions and customs, but we can see that in the New Testament, the Bible encourages us to *Let every man be fully persuaded in his own mind.* In light of arguments both for and against the principles of tithing and giving under the New covenant, I encourage you to do the same.

Let me give you an example of how God encouraged me to give. I meet with a group of ministers each month, and one of the pastors flew his plane down. The pastor made it known that he needed fuel for the plane to return. So the ministers got together and agreed to give to him. I had $130 in my pocket. Now for some reason God was purposing upon my heart to give the $100, but I was purposing in my heart to give $30. I was watching the others to see how much they were giving, but God didn't want me to give based on what others were giving, He wanted me to do what He'd purposed me to do. When the plate came around, I gave $30, which was still going beyond what others gave. But God tapped me on the shoulder and said, "Now I told you to give a hundred."

Afterward we went out to eat and I was uncomfortable because of God tugging at my heart. You know how God won't let you rest. I was eating and God said, "I told you to give the hundred." What was I going to do? I sat there and we were eating and talking; and I couldn't really talk well because something was wrong. God was convicting me so I gave in.

Now in my mind I wondered if I could ask him to give me the $30 back, and I would give him the hundred. You see I needed the money for gas and to pay for my food. I kept thinking how I was going to do this. And the Lord said, "You should have been obedient the first time, so now you need to give it all now because it is unethical for you to ask for your money back. Had you been obedient from the beginning you would have had $30 in your pocket."

When we got through eating and everyone was saying goodbye, I grabbed the pastor by the hand and said, "Would it be a problem if I were to sow a second time into your life?" I told him I needed to be obedient, because the Lord was whooping up on me. I shook his hand and gave him the $100. He didn't look at it; he just put it into his pocket. But I was obedient. While he was sitting down he said, "Pastor Washington, we have a house and the church is going to be selling the house. I'm impressed to give you the tithe off the profit of the house." Give God some praise.

I humbly said, "Amen." He said, "Pastor Washington, the house is worth over $300,000." I said, "Hallelujah!" Do you see how beneficial it is to be obedient in sowing the seed that God has purposed in your heart?

The Bible says, *And God is able to make all grace abound toward you; that ye, always having all sufficiency in all things, may abound to every good work.* When we give, His power unleashes all grace to be abundant for us so that we can be abundant in every good work. This passage is talking about giving and serving others. We would not be able to help others without the supply of God's grace. This grace is not necessarily spiritual grace but it is referring to material necessity. In other words it says, "God is able to make all money or material necessities abound toward you." God is able to keep you and sustain you in spite of your financial condition. I'm telling you that God is able to make all grace abound towards you; that you always having ALL sufficiency in ALL things may abound to every good work. In other words, God wants you to be blessed so that you can continue to work for Him. Amen? That's blessing.

Having all sufficiency means having more than enough. God wants you to always have more than enough, so that in all things you may abound to every good work *as it is written he has dispersed abroad, he had given to the poor, his righteousness remaineth forever.* God gives to everybody; He has dispersed abroad, and His righteousness remains forever. Out of His righteousness and out of His love He gives.

Now he that ministereth seed to the sower both minister bread for your food, and multiply your seed sown, and increase the fruits of your righteousness;) Being enriched in every thing to all bountifulness, which causeth through us thanksgiving to God.

God is letting us know that He is the one who feeds us, not our jobs, not our friends or family, and not ourselves—it is God. God will multiply the fruit of our seed sown on behalf of Him and increase the fruits of your righteousness. In other words, giving brings increase to your testimony as a Christian.

We will also be *enriched in everything to all bountifulness which causes through us thanksgiving to God. For the administration of this service not only supplieth the want of the saints, but is abundant also by many thanksgivings unto God; Whiles by the experiment of this ministration they glorify God for your professed subjection unto the gospel of Christ, and for your liberal distribution unto them, and unto all men.* [2 Corinthians 9:8-13]

Paul was writing to the Corinthian church and he was trying to get them to make a collection to give to the Jerusalem church. Paul was encouraging them to send an offering to the church of Jerusalem, who had fallen on bad times and bad ground. They needed money. What better way to show them the love of God than to sow a seed to help them. He goes on to say that their offering would cause them to be thankful to God. God would be glorified through their giving.

> **Did You Know?**
>
> When a man's ways please the LORD, he maketh even his enemies to be at peace with him.
>
> —Proverbs 16:7

God Himself is our greatest example. He always gives. There have been times when we have been on the wrong side of the tracks doing the wrong thing. During these times, who do we call on? We call on God, don't we? In the midst of our storms, He always comes through.

The spiritual law of giving is if you give, it shall be given back to you. If you keep your hand closed and be stingy, that's what you are going to get back. In fact people are going to give you what you give them. Jesus said, *For with the same measure that ye mete withal it shall be measured to you again.* [Luke 6:38]

The law of giving is a spiritual law that operates

like any law God has created. We can use the natural law of gravity as an example. If you drop something it's going to fall. But we also know that while the law of gravity is constant—in that gravity exerts the same force upon an object regardless of its size, weight, or mass—there are factors that affect the speed of a falling object—friction for example. God is encouraging us to give, and if we do, just like an object, we will see results. However, like the law of gravity, our motives behind giving act like friction, which can, if not correct, hinder the speed and force of the falling object. Likewise, a correct heart in giving will produce better results. In other words, your motivation is equally as important as your giving.

The Lord is challenging all of us today. No one is exempt from giving. The spiritual law says that if we do give God will give back to us. Put Him to the test. Put God to the test. That's what His word says.

chapter 8

Key to Answered Prayers

And I will give unto you the keys to the kingdom of heaven: and whatsoever thou shalt bind on earth shall be bound in heaven; and whatsoever thou shalt loose on earth shall be loosed in heaven. [Matthew 16:19]

While the primary focus of this book is to teach about the benefits of the firstfruits, it is important for you to understand that there are other variables that may affect God's blessings being experienced in your life. Let us remember what Jesus said concerning paying tithes, *Woe unto you, scribes and Pharisees, hypocrites! for ye pay tithe of mint and anise and cummin, and have omitted the weightier matters of the law, judgment, mercy, and faith: these ought ye to have done, and not to leave the other undone.* [Matthew 23:23]

Jesus is teaching that paying tithes is done in conjunction with other matters of faith, and ignoring these other matters can affect your receiving of God's blessings. This is similar to the point I made concerning the law of gravity. The law of gravity is constant in that it exerts a continuous force upon every object, but the way an object reacts to gravity is dependent upon variables like mass, weight, and friction. This is why I want to give you a key that God has designed to work in conjunction with the firstfruits. You can give and tithe all you want and you may see some results, but in order to reap the fullness of God's benefits, this key must be used.

Keys represent authority and access. If you want to get into a room that has a locked door, all you need is a key. If we had the key to getting our prayers answered, all we would have to do is use it. Jesus said, *I will give unto you the keys to the kingdom of heaven...* [Matthew 16:19] I want to stress this point... that Jesus gave us keys (plural), not a singular key or solution to accessing God's kingdom. However, it is one thing to have keys, but just having the keys doesn't get you into the room. You have to use them; and use them correctly.

In addition to giving us the keys to the kingdom of heaven, the Lord also teaches us how to utilize these keys to gain access to God's kingdom and the inheritance we have in Christ. In this chapter, I'm going to discuss an important key that will unlock the door to your prayers becoming a reality. I will base this key on the assumption that you already have revelation of what the Bible teaches concerning faith and access into God's grace. *By whom also we have access by faith into this grace wherein we stand and rejoice in hope of the glory of God.* [Romans 5:2] Furthermore, I will stipulate that you also know that faith works by love (Galatians 5:6). Therefore, the key we will discuss will not profit you without having a solid foundation and understanding of faith and love. You can learn more about how faith and love work in 1 Corinthians 13:1-3.

The Power of Forgiveness

And Jesus answering saith unto them, Have faith in God. For verily I say unto you, That whosoever shall say unto this mountain, Be thou removed, and be thou cast into the sea; and shall not doubt in his heart, but shall believe that those things which he saith shall come to pass; he shall have whatsoever he saith. Therefore I say unto you, What things soever ye desire, when ye pray, believe that ye receive them, and ye shall have them. And when ye stand praying, forgive, if ye have ought against any: that your Father also which is in heaven may forgive you your tres-

passes. But if ye do not forgive, neither will your Father which is in heaven forgive your trespasses. [Mark 11:22-26]

There is probably no greater hindrance to receiving God's blessings than a person who lives in unforgiveness toward others. In this passage, the Lord relates forgiveness to not only faith, but to receiving the answers to your prayers. As you will see, unforgiveness hinders a person's faith to receive, which stops the flow of these answers.

Jesus begins this teaching on the prayer of faith by stressing the focus of a person's faith, *Have faith in God.* Then, He explains a great truth about prayer, *Therefore I say unto you, What things soever ye desire, when ye pray, believe that ye receive them, and ye shall have them.* Faith requires that you must believe *when ye pray* that you have received the answer to your prayers. Jesus did not say that you must believe once you have received. Rather, the Lord instructs us to believe *when we pray* in order to have them. This

Tithing Tips

10¢

of every dollar is all God asks of you.

is a foundational truth of faith, but yet it is rarely practiced, which may explain why we aren't seeing many of our prayers answered. The laws of faith also require an expectation of a positive response. Confidence in God's faithfulness to His word is a frequent topic in Scripture. The apostle John wrote, *And this is the confidence that we have in him, that, if we ask anything according to his will, he hears us. And if we know that he hears us, whatsoever we ask, we know that we have the petitions that we desired of him.* [1 John 5:14-15]

Hebrews 10:35-38 says, *Cast not away therefore your confidence, which hath great recompense of reward. For ye have need of patience, that, after ye have done the will of God, ye might receive the promise. For yet a little while, and he that shall come will come, and will not tarry. Now the just shall live by faith: but if any man draw back, my soul shall have no pleasure in him.*

So, as Jesus teaches us about faith, He inserts an important key into the mix: forgiveness. *And when ye stand praying, forgive, if ye have ought against any: that your Father also which is in heaven may forgive you your trespasses. But if ye do not forgive, neither will your Father which is in heaven forgive your trespasses.*

Jesus is teaching that unforgiveness blocks or hinders the flow of God's power, promises, and blessings toward us. Jesus said, *What things soever ye desire, when ye pray, believe that ye receive them, and ye shall have them.* He is saying that all of our desires will be given to us when we pray in faith. Picture a large pipe with God's blessings on one end and you on the other. By grace, God has ordered His blessings to flow through this pipe, so we know the blessings are flowing. However, in the middle of this pipe is a valve that governs the flow of blessings, and this valve is called "Forgiveness". In other words, a person can pray with all faith, according to the will of God, but if he is living in unforgiveness, this valve will be closed, blocking off the flow of God's power.

Although many people believe God to be the variable in this case, this is not so. God is never the variable concerning His promises. The Bible says, *Do not err, my beloved brethren. Every good gift and every perfect gift is from above, and cometh down from the Father of lights, with whom is no variableness, neither shadow of turning.* [James 1:16-17]

This says that God is not the variable concerning His good and perfect gifts and neither is there any sign or shadow of turning or repenting of these gifts.

The Bible also says, *For the gifts and calling of God are without repentance.* [Romans 11:29]

> **Did You Know?**
>
> Jesus taught about paying tithes:
>
> **Matthew 10:10**
> **Matthew 23:23**
> **Mark 12:15-17**
> **Mark 12:41-44**
> **Luke 10:7-8**
> **Luke 11:42**

Therefore, when the Lord says, *But if ye do not forgive, neither will your Father which is in heaven forgive your trespasses,* He is not saying that God is the one withholding His blessing or favor toward you, because then God's forgiveness would be dependent upon our works. This violates the comprehensive teaching of grace in the New Testament. In fact, it is because of God's forgiveness, that the Lord commands us to forgive. We cannot give away something we have never received. Therefore, it is impossible to forgive others as we have been forgiven until we have revelation of God's forgiveness.

If you were to ask what work of God would require the most faith, most people would point to a miracle or healing. However, we know that the disciples healed many sick people, cast out demons, and raised people from the dead, but yet on only one occasion did they ask the Lord for more faith—and it was when Jesus was teaching on forgiveness.

Then said he unto the disciples, It is impossible but that offences will come: but woe unto him, through whom they come! It were better for him that a millstone were hanged about his neck, and he cast into the sea, than that he should offend one of these little ones. Take heed to yourselves: If thy brother trespass against thee, rebuke him; and if he repent, forgive him. And if he trespass against thee seven times in a day, and seven times in a day turn again to thee, saying, I repent; thou shalt forgive him. And the apostles said unto the Lord, Increase our faith. And the Lord said, If ye had faith as a grain of mustard seed, ye might say unto this sycamine tree, Be thou plucked up by the root, and be thou planted in the sea; and it should obey you. [Luke 17:1-6]

Although a person doesn't need any more faith to forgive, as Jesus would teach in the succeeding verses in Luke's gospel, we see that forgiveness is a difficult concept to practice because it involves us dealing with our flesh and emotions. However, unforgiveness results in much of the grief we experience in this world. It is amazing that in light of how God has forgiven us for our sins against Him, that we continue to harbor grudges against people. I believe this is because we have failed to understand the extent of how we've been forgiven. If we were to get a revelation of the depths of our sins and how offensive sin is in God's eyes, and then to see the extreme high price Jesus paid to actually become sin for us, perhaps we would be more inclined to forgive. What seems to be a gross offense to us is a grain of sand in comparison to our sins against God. Jesus teaches this principle in response to a question from Peter about forgiveness:

Then came Peter to him, and said, Lord, how oft shall my brother sin against me, and I forgive him? till seven times? Jesus saith unto him, I say not unto thee, Until seven times: but, Until seventy times seven. Therefore is the kingdom of heaven likened unto a certain king, which would take account of his servants. And when he had begun to reckon, one was brought unto him, which owed him ten thousand talents. But forasmuch as he had not to pay, his lord commanded him to be sold, and his wife, and children, and all that he had, and payment to be made. The servant therefore fell down, and worshipped him, saying, Lord, have patience with me, and I will pay thee all. Then the lord of that servant was moved with compassion, and loosed him, and forgave him the debt.

But the same servant went out, and found one of his fellowservants, which owed him an hundred pence: and he laid hands on him, and took him by the throat, saying, Pay me that thou owest. And his fellowservant fell down at his feet, and besought him, saying, Have patience with me, and I will pay thee all. And he would not: but went and cast him into prison, till he should pay the debt.

So when his fellowservants saw what was done, they were very sorry, and came and told unto their lord all that was done. Then his lord, after that he had called him, said unto him, O thou wicked servant, I forgave thee all that debt, because thou desiredst me: Shouldest not thou also have had compassion on thy fellowservant, even as I had pity on thee? And his lord was wroth, and delivered him to the tormentors, till he should pay all that was due unto him. So likewise shall my heavenly Father do also unto you, if ye from your hearts forgive not every one his brother their trespasses. [Matthew 18:23-35]

The servant to whom the Lord is referring was forgiven a great debt by his lord, but after being forgiven, the same servant refused to extend mercy to someone who owed him a very small debt. This parable is a picture of the tremendous debt we owed God for sin, but at the same time, it tells us the consequences when we refuse to forgive others who have done things that are insignificant in comparison. Jesus said that a person who does not forgive after being forgiven will be delivered to the tormentors.

Again, the Lord is not saying that God in essence would unleash the devil on people, but rather, unforgive-ness opens the door to the devil and his torment. The Bible teaches this principle in several places. The apostle Paul instructs the Corinthian church to extend forgiveness and restoration to the man in sin about whom he wrote in an earlier letter (1 Corinthians 5).

So that contrariwise ye ought rather to forgive him, and comfort him, lest perhaps such a one should be swallowed up with overmuch sorrow. Wherefore I beseech you that ye would confirm your love toward him. For to this end also did I write, that I might know the proof of you, whether ye be obedient in all things. To whom ye forgive any thing, I forgive also: for if I forgave any thing, to whom I forgave it, for your sakes forgave I it in the person of Christ; Lest

Satan should get an advantage of us: for we are not ignorant of his devices. [2 Corinthians 2:7-11]

Paul is teaching that unforgiveness is a device or tool the devil uses to destroy us. Paul also makes this same exhortation to the church at Ephesus: *Be ye angry, and sin not: let not the sun go down upon your wrath: Neither give place to the devil. Let him that stole steal no more: but rather let him labour, working with his hands the thing which is good, that he may have to give to him that needeth. Let no corrupt communication proceed out of your mouth, but that which is good to the use of edifying, that it may minister grace unto the hearers. And grieve not the holy Spirit of God, whereby ye are sealed unto the day of redemption. Let all bitterness, and wrath, and anger, and clamour, and evil speaking, be put away from you, with all malice: And be ye kind one to another, tenderhearted, forgiving one another, even as God for Christ's sake hath forgiven you.* [Ephesians 4:26-32]

Again, the apostle Paul stresses the fact that we should forgive as a byproduct of receiving God's forgiveness. He makes a similar statement to the Colossians: *Put on therefore, as*

BENEFITS

God will open the windows of Heaven and pour blessings upon you. (Malachi 3:10) *the elect of God, holy and beloved, bowels of mercies, kindness, humbleness of mind, meekness, longsuffering; Forbearing one another, and forgiving one another, if any man have a quarrel against any: even as Christ forgave you, so also do ye.* [Colossians 3:12-13]

Walking in unforgiveness can keep back a lot of blessings that the Lord has for us. Our flesh tells us that holding a grudge gives us power, when in fact, the opposite is true. When we do not forgive and hold grudges, we relinquish any power we had and give it to the devil. In forgiving others, you are in the driver's seat, but when you refuse to forgive, you allow the object of your grudge to exercise power over you—to control you.

Forgiveness is a choice you make that benefits you—not necessarily the person who has wronged you. It frees you from the poison that bitterness brings. Therefore, it is critical that you forgive others in order to see the fullness of God's blessings in your life.

This is only one key among the many God has given us to access the kingdom of Heaven. He has given you authority to bind and loose—start loosing today through forgiveness. You hold the key!

How Do I Change My Situation?

chapter

9

And I will give unto you the keys to the kingdom of heaven: and whatsoever thou shalt bind on earth shall be bound in heaven; and whatsoever thou shalt loose on earth shall be loosed in heaven. [Matthew 16:19]

Because the principles of the firstfruits seem to be illogical to the natural mind, often unbelief will cause a person to disregard the importance of tithing, and consequently miss out on the benefits of investing in God's kingdom. As we saw in Proverbs 3:9 that says, *Honour the LORD with thy substance, and with the firstfruits of all thine increase,* tithing is a way of honoring God. The Bible teaches us a way of seeking God that can combat against unbelief; and this is through fasting.

The Benefits of Fasting

Do you want to change some things in your life? In the previous chapter, we discussed how forgiveness is a key to seeing the answers to your prayers come to pass. While unforgiveness can hinder a person's faith from operating, there are other obstacles to receiving the blessings of God, and the primary one of these is unbelief. Because forgiveness is an act of the will and of the heart, our flesh often gets in the way. In the same way that unforgiveness is of the flesh so also is unbelief.

The word of God gives us a useful tool in combating the flesh, which will promote forgiveness and also minimize unbelief in your life. This tool is fasting. Fasting was practiced in the Old Testament as a means of afflicting your flesh and consecrating yourself before God. In the New Testament, the same standard is applied, but always in light of the atonement Jesus has made and the grace that has already been given to us. A fast is not a hunger strike or other manipulative means to make God "move" on your behalf, as some practice. Fasting doesn't change God, the devil, or your circumstances. Rather, fasting deals with the unbelief that is present in your flesh or soul. In other words, fasting changes you so you can get God's power flowing toward you.

Fasting has long been viewed as a religious observance and the religious Jews in Jesus' day saw fasting in this same light. As with many things, the Lord used the actions of the hypocritical religious people to teach us what *not* to do while, at the same time, teaching us the true purpose of these important principles.

Moreover when ye fast, be not, as the hypocrites, of a sad countenance: for they disfigure their faces, that they may appear unto men to fast. Verily I say unto you, They have their reward. But thou, when thou fastest, anoint thine head, and wash thy face; That thou appear not unto men to fast, but unto thy Father which is in secret: and thy Father, which seeth in secret, shall reward thee openly. [Matthew 6:16-18]

Jesus is teaching us that the religious Jews practiced fasting in order to receive acclaim and praise from men. Because of their appearance, it would be obvious they were fasting, and perhaps they were bragging about it as well. They wanted a pat on the back from man rather than using the fast as a way of seeking the honor that comes from God only. Jesus tied this behavior to faith when He said, *How can ye believe, which receive honour one of another, and seek not the honour that cometh from God only?* [John 5:44]

> **Did You Know?**
>
> Everyone is equal when it comes to tithes. The rich and poor give the same —10%.

In various places, the Bible teaches us not to be

man pleasers because the only reward from this is the praise of man, which is temporary, while the honor that comes from God is eternal. Similar to His teaching on prayer (Matthew 6:5-6), the Lord instructs us to fast in secret so that the Father would reward us openly, for everyone to see. The apostle Paul encouraged Timothy in this same light when it came to seeking God. He said, *Meditate upon these things; give thyself wholly to them; that thy profiting may appear to all.* [1 Timothy 4:15]

While the Lord taught us what to do and how to act when we fast, there is little teaching of the principles of fasting and what fasting is to accomplish. We see that the church in Antioch fasted, prayed, and ministered to the Lord, which resulted in the sending out of Paul and Barnabas on their first missionary journey (Acts 13:1-3). It appears that the consecration of prayer, fasting, and ministering to the Lord opened their hearts wide to hear the Lord's voice.

Fasting For Unbelief

This is a two-pronged teaching. Fasting and prayer strengthens faith and reduces unbelief, while at the same time deals with certain *kinds* of demonic forces—that some kind of devils *goeth not out but by prayer and fasting*. I'll cover fasting against demons in the next section. In terms of how fasting deals with unbelief and problems of the flesh, there is only one teaching from the New Testament, and it is found in the gospels when Jesus returned from the Mount of Transfiguration. We will examine both Matthew and Mark's account to get the entire scope of this teaching. Matthew writes:

And when they were come to the multitude, there came to him a certain man, kneeling down to him, and saying, Lord, have mercy on my son: for he is a lunatic, and sore vexed: for ofttimes he falleth into the fire, and oft into the water. And I brought him to thy disciples, and they could not cure him. Then Jesus answered and said, O faithless and perverse generation, how long shall I be with you? how long shall I suffer you? bring him hither to me. And Jesus rebuked the devil; and he departed out of him: and the child was cured from that very hour. Then came the disciples to Jesus apart, and said, Why could not we cast him out? And Jesus said unto them, Because of your unbelief: for verily I say unto you, If ye have faith as a grain of mustard seed, ye shall say unto this mountain, Remove hence to yonder place; and it shall remove; and nothing shall be impossible unto you. Howbeit this kind goeth not out but by prayer and fasting. [Matthew 17:14-21]

In this account, Jesus tied the disciples' inability

to cast out the demon to unbelief (verse 20). And this is where the Lord is teaching us concerning how fasting and prayer affects our unbelief. Let's read what Mark writes about the same encounter:

And when he came to his disciples, he saw a great multitude about them, and the scribes questioning with them. And straightway all the people, when they beheld him, were greatly amazed, and running to him saluted him. And he asked the scribes, What question ye with them? And one of the multitude answered and said, Master, I have brought unto thee my son, which hath a dumb spirit; And wheresoever he taketh him, he teareth him: and he foameth, and gnasheth with his teeth, and pineth away: and I spake to thy disciples that they should cast him out; and they could not. He answereth him, and saith, O faithless generation, how long shall I be with you? how long shall I suffer you? bring him unto me. And they brought him unto him: and when he saw him, straightway the spirit tare him; and he fell on the ground, and wallowed foaming. And he asked his father, How long is it ago since this came unto him? And he said, Of a child. And ofttimes it hath cast him into the fire, and into the waters, to destroy him: but if thou canst do any thing, have compassion on us, and help us. Jesus said unto him, If thou canst believe, all things are possible to him that believeth. And straightway the father of the child cried out, and said with tears, Lord, I believe; help thou mine unbelief. When Jesus saw that the people came running together, he rebuked the foul spirit, saying unto him, Thou dumb and deaf spirit, I charge thee, come out of him, and enter no more into him. And the spirit cried, and rent him sore, and came out of him: and he was as one dead; insomuch that many said, He is dead. But Jesus took him by the hand, and lifted him up; and he arose. And when he was come into the house, his disciples asked him privately, Why could not we cast him out? And he said unto them, This kind can come forth by nothing, but by prayer and fasting. [Mark 9:14-23]

You're going to have some people in your midst that are not going to be able to do some of the things you desire them to do. Here the disciples who walked with Jesus; who talked with Jesus; who slept with Jesus; and ate with Jesus, yet they weren't able to change the situation. The man let Jesus know that the disciples couldn't help him. Jesus said, "O, faithless generation."

In order to change your situation you're going to have to be faithful. He said, *Faithless generation, how long shall I be with you? How long shall I suffer you?*

Bring him to me. I'm glad that we can bring our situation to Him. The question is: are we bringing our situation to the Master? We might call up Susie and tell her about our situation, or go on the job and tell them about our situation, and then we'll be arguing about what they could or could not do. Jesus said, *O faithless generation bring him to me.* There's hope.

And they brought him unto him; and when he saw him, straightway the spirit tare him; and he fell on the ground and wallowed foaming. I want you to know that when you bring your situation to Him, the enemy is going to get mad, and more than likely your situation is going to get worse. Even in the face of Jesus—standing before the answer himself the situation got worse. That man's son got worse standing before the Messiah. *"And he asked his father, How long is it ago since this came unto him?"* It seems to us that we want Jesus to go ahead and start the work, don't we? But Jesus would like to talk a little bit to find out what happened. What did you expose yourself to? What did you do that has placed you in this situation? Before I begin to heal it, before I begin to deliver it, I want to talk to you.

And he said of a child. In other words a long time ago. *And oftentimes it hath cast him into the fire, and into the waters to destroy him; but if thou canst do any thing.* Sometimes we just want God just to do something. It's as if we're saying, "You don't have to heal the whole thing but just let me see something. I mean if you can do anything, just do something." When you bring your situation to Christ you start this dialog with Him. He's not only working outwardly but He's working inwardly so that you won't be caught back in the same situation tomorrow. If He would just heal it outwardly tomorrow you'd be at His feet again, saying, "Help me, I'm in the same situation." Jesus said, "Let's talk a little while and find out what happened, and see what we can do about it."

The man tells Jesus about the situation, how long it was and how bad it was. And then he says, *But if thou canst do any thing, have compassion on us, and help us.* Jesus said unto him, *If thou canst believe.* Jesus already had this conversation with him and now Jesus is dealing with the man's faith. He has come to the conclusion that perhaps his faith is on trial and perhaps he needs his faith to be revived and strengthened. And Jesus said, *If thou canst believe, all things are possible to him that believeth.* Jesus said, *All things are possible.* Some of us do not believe that all things are possible. We have to get that in our hearts. No matter how bleak, how dim, or how dark the situation looks, Jesus says, *All things are possible.*

Had it been you or I sitting in a desperate situation with our son on the ground foaming at the mouth and the situation had escalated, how would we react? We probably would be shaking our fists in the air saying, "Fix this now, we'll talk later, please. My boy is over here foaming; you can't really get my undivided attention, and I know you are sharing with me about faith, but my boy is foaming at the mouth and the enemy has the advantage over him; and God, we can talk later, please. Can you go ahead and fix this situation?"

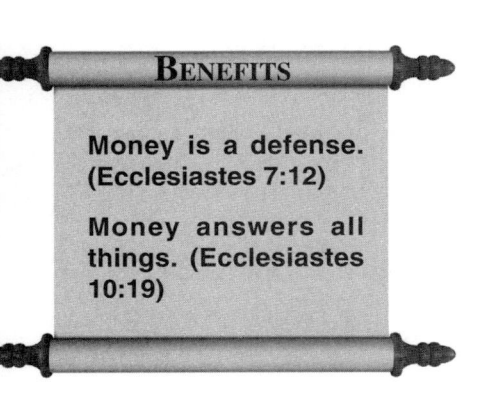

I tell you the Lord will come on His time, and often times the reason why our situation has not changed is because we have not accepted the dialog between He and us. We really haven't sat down to talk to the Master about it because of the many issues going on. We'd rather turn and walk the other way. *And straightway the father of the child cried out and*

> **BENEFITS**
>
> Money is a defense. (Ecclesiastes 7:12)
>
> Money answers all things. (Ecclesiastes 10:19)

said with tears, Lord, I believe; help thou mine unbelief!

It's as if he were saying, "I'm having problems believing all the way. I believe that you're awesome; I believe that you can do anything. I believe that you are the Alpha and the Omega, the beginning and the end. But I'm having problems believing that you can help me in this situation right now. I know that You shed Your blood on Calvary, but I'm having a little problem believing that You can help me right now in my situation."

This man was wise when he asked for help to believe that Jesus would heal his son. No one but Jesus could help him. *When Jesus saw that the people came running together, he rebuked the foul spirit, and said unto him, Thou dumb and deaf spirit, I charge thee to come out of him and enter no more into him.* With the authority and power of God, Jesus began to change the outcome of the situation immediately. Jesus took control of the situation. The Scripture says; *But Jesus took him by the hand and lifted him up; and he arose.* His situation changed, didn't it? It seemed like it was made worse, but then Jesus lifted him and he arose. That's exactly what we need—is for Jesus to come by and lift us out of our present situation. He can and will through prayer and fasting.

And when he was coming into the house, his disciples asked him privately, Why could not we cast him out? And he said unto them, This kind can come forth by nothing, but by prayer and fasting. Have you ever wondered why things happen in your life? Some people say, "Don't question the Lord." I believe it's all right to ask the Lord why. The Lord is waiting on you to ask the question, so he can give you the answer. The Bible says, *If any of you lack wisdom, let him ask of God, that giveth to all men liberally, and upbraideth not; and it shall be given him.* [James 1:5]

The disciples' question was, *Why could not we cast him out?* How can I change my situation? is maybe the question you're asking now. *And he said unto them, This kind can come forth by nothing, but by prayer and fasting.* In other words, your situation can and will change, through prayer and fasting.

You've got the answer to your problem now. The Lord just gave you the answer to your problem. Don't you want to change? You've been praying, and pleading the blood. You've been doing everything you know but it hasn't brought about the expected results. Sometimes you can pray and get a breakthrough and you can see the manifestation right before you get out of the house. But there are other times when it doesn't work that way.

You expect God to move and you wonder why hasn't the situation changed. Jesus gives us the answer: He said "this kind cometh forth by prayer and fasting."

Jesus is saying, "I want you to be a part of this breakthrough. I'm not going to do all of the work. I'm going to cause you to lay your flesh on the altar. Now you're going to have to turn the plate down, lay yourself on the altar and if I see the sacrifice I'll come running to you. If I see you pleading the blood in your own flesh, putting your flesh under subjection and turning down the plate, then I'll know that I'm important to you."

When you fast, God will know that the issue at hand is very desperate. I believe there are different kinds of unbelief and that fasting and prayer deals with a natural unbelief that comes from living by our senses for so long. Fasting is the training ground for our flesh to submit to the will of the Spirit. When you fast, it is a sacrifice unto the Lord because your body starts talking to you saying, "I'm hungry and I want to be fed, and if you don't feed me, I'm going to make your head hurt. I'm going to make your stomach growl." Your flesh will rebel against your decision to fast; your flesh will declare war against you.

Because your flesh or senses have basically ruled over your life for so long, they act like a spoiled child when they don't get what they want. The flesh is accustomed to getting its demands met, and because this kind of unbelief comes from the senses, fasting trains your flesh to believe the word of God that says, *It is written, Man shall not live by bread alone, but by every word that proceedeth out of the mouth of God.* [Matthew 4:4]

The desire for food is one of the strongest desires of the body; and especially in this country, it is often the most indulged. Most Americans live to eat rather than eat to live. Although fasting can involve abstinence from many things, it is most effective when it involves food. Fasting tells the body that the Spirit is in control; and places the body under subjection to the Spirit and word of God. The apostle Paul writes of this, *But I keep under my body, and bring it into subjection: lest that by any means, when I have preached to others, I myself should be a castaway.* [1 Corinthians 9:27]

Especially as it relates to healing of sickness and disease, fasting accompanied by prayer (seeking God) trains the flesh to respond in a positive way to what the word of God says. The person who doesn't have his flesh under subjection to the Spirit will not get the results he wants because once he speaks to his flesh to be healed, his flesh will respond, "Who are you? I tell you what to do—not the other way around."

But the person who has his flesh under control, as self-control is a fruit of the Spirit (Galatians 5:23) he will get much better results, especially as it relates to physical manifestation.

Fasting Against Demons

Although Jesus tied the disciples' inability to cast out the demon to unbelief, I believe his reference to fasting also applied to their power against certain demonic forces that may be stronger than others. Jesus said that some demons are stronger than others (Matthew 12:45). When the Lord said, *Howbeit this kind*, I believe He is referring to *this kind* of devil. We can see this from Mark's account:

And when he was come into the house, his disciples asked him privately, Why could not we cast him out? And he said unto them, This kind can come forth by nothing, but by prayer and fasting. [Mark 9:28-29]

One Bible scholar asserts, "...that a certain class or genus of demons cannot be expelled but by prayer and fasting, while others may be ejected without them... there are certain evil propensities, in some persons, which pampering the flesh tends to nourish and strengthen; and that self-denial and fasting, accompanied by prayer to God, are the most likely means, not only to mortify such propensities, but also to destroy them."

In his Bible commentary, Matthew Henry writes, "Though the adversaries we wrestle, be all principalities and powers, yet some are stronger than others, and their power more hardly broken. Fasting and prayer are proper means for the bringing down of Satan's power against us, and the fetching in of divine power to our assistance."

Another commentator adds: "With God all things are equally possible; but to us, one devil may be harder to deal with than another. One kind will go at a word, but of others it may be said, "This kind goeth not out but by prayer and fasting." He that would overcome the devil in certain instances must first overcome heaven by prayer and conquer himself by self-denial. The drink devil is of the kind, which may assuredly be conquered by faith; and yet we must generally use much intercession God-ward, and total abstinence, as an example man-ward, before we can displace this demon."

The disciples had the power to cast out demons (Matthew 10:1,8) and had also successfully cast out many demons prior to this occasion (Luke 10:17), but apparently this kind of demon, in light of its physical manifestation in the boy, was stronger and required the use of fasting to deal with it.

We can see this in a case of a person who's under the influence of a strong spirit, one of drug addiction, for example. Because of its strength, it may take prayer and fasting to overcome him in comparison to a "weaker" spirit.

Fasting For Understanding

In addition to dealing with unbelief, we can also see that seeking God through prayer and fasting can accomplish things that relate to understanding of God's word. Daniel is an example of someone who sought to understand God's will and purposes for his people Israel. Therefore, he used a combination of prayer and fasting to remove any distractions from his flesh and mind that would hinder his understanding of God's will.

In the first year of Darius the son of Ahasuerus, of the seed of the Medes, which was made king over the realm of the Chaldeans; In the first year of his reign I Daniel understood by books the number of the years, whereof the word of the LORD came to Jeremiah the prophet, that he would accomplish seventy years in the desolations of Jerusalem. And I set my face unto the Lord God, to seek by prayer and supplications, with fasting, and sackcloth, and ashes: [Daniel 9:1-3]

Daniel was seeking God based on a promise the Lord made to Israel through the prophet Jeremiah—that after seventy years of captivity in Babylon, Israel would return to their land and rebuild Jerusalem. The time had been fulfilled and Daniel was seeking of the Lord, how this was going to be accomplished. In other words, he was seeking God to understand what He had already promised. He wasn't asking God to move; but rather, to let him understand the word that had been given.

After reciting the prayer he made to God, he tells us what happened as a result:

> **Tithing Tips**
>
> Statistics show that only 2% of church members tithe 100% of the time. Imagine a church where every member tithed 100% of the time. No one would lack. Are you in this 2%? If not, why?

And whiles I was speaking, and praying, and confessing my sin and the sin of my people Israel, and presenting my supplication before the LORD my God for the holy mountain of my God; Yea, whiles I was speaking in prayer, even the man Gabriel, whom I had seen in the vision at the beginning, being caused to fly swiftly, touched me about the time of the evening oblation. And he informed me, and talked with me, and said, O Daniel, I am now come forth to give thee skill and understanding. At the beginning of thy supplications the commandment came forth, and I am come to show thee; for thou art greatly beloved: therefore understand the matter, and consider the vision. [Daniel 9:20-23]

Herein this passage is a great truth. While Daniel was still praying, the answer to his prayer arrived in the form of the angel Gabriel. Gabriel said, *At the beginning of thy supplications the commandment came forth.* Daniel was heard at the beginning—when he set his face to seek the Lord; and didn't even finish his prayer. Daniel's prayer was a prayer of faith, consisting of remembering God's faithfulness to keep the words of His covenant (verse 4) and relying upon the mercies of God—and not on their own righteousness (verse 18) to see the promise come to pass. The Bible teaches us to ask according to God's revealed word in expectation of a positive answer (1 John 5:14-15). In other words, don't cancel out your faith by saying, "If it be thy will."

Gabriel informed Daniel that he had come to give him skill and understanding; and it was because

Daniel had consecrated himself through fasting, he was able to understand God's promise clearly. This is a great example of the Scripture that says, *Then shall ye call upon me, and ye shall go and pray unto me, and I will hearken unto you. And ye shall seek me, and find me, when ye shall search for me with all your heart. And I will be found of you, saith the LORD: and I will turn away your captivity, and I will gather you from all the nations, and from all the places whither I have driven you, saith the LORD; and I will bring you again into the place whence I caused you to be carried away captive.* [Jeremiah 29:12-14]

Don't we need to have skill and understanding? The Bible says to get wisdom and in thy getting, get understanding (Proverbs 4:7). If an angel gives you understanding, you have the answer. Understanding, in this context, refers to revelation of God's will. In the New Testament, this was the prayer of the apostle Paul for the believers in Ephesus:

That the God of our Lord Jesus Christ, the Father of glory, may give unto you the spirit of wisdom and revelation in the knowledge of him: The eyes of your understanding being enlightened; that ye may know... [Ephesians 1:17-18]

It is evident because of Daniel's reference to what God had revealed to Jeremiah, that Daniel followed God's instructions how to seek the fulfillment of the promise He made to Israel. Through fasting and prayer, Daniel was seeking God with his whole heart.

Many of you are seeking skill and understanding of your situation, and how to change things in your life. You may be in captivity by your own mistakes and want to understand how to get free. We have the model from Daniel to temporarily remove yourself from all the distractions of this world and set your face to seek God. Fasting or abstaining from the "things of the world" puts your full attention—your whole heart—on God and the answers to your issues. God has all answers and all wisdom, but these things are received only through diligent seeking of God as the Bible says, *But without faith it is impossible to please him: for he that cometh to God must believe that he is, and that he is a rewarder of them that diligently seek him.* [Hebrews 11:6]

So what does the Lord want us to know today? He wants us to seek Him with our whole heart. We need to fast. We need to remove ourselves from the world daily to seek God and an understanding of His will. The Bible says, *Wherefore be ye not unwise, but understanding what the will of the Lord is.* [Ephesians 5:17]

We also need to do what the Scripture says and offer our bodies as a living sacrifice on the altar of the Lord. The Bible says, *I beseech you therefore, brethren, by the mercies of God, that ye present your bodies a living sacrifice, holy, acceptable unto God, which is your reasonable service. And be not conformed to this world: but be ye transformed by the renewing of your mind, that ye may prove what is that good, and acceptable, and perfect, will of God.* [Romans 12:1-2]

> **Did You Know?**
>
> Fasting Will...
>
> - undo heavy burdens
> - break the band of wickedness
> - let the oppressed go free
> - your health will spring forth speedily
> - break the yokes
> - God will satisfy you in drought
>
> and more... Isaiah 58:6-11

By offering your bodies as a living sacrifice to God and the renewing of your minds through God's word, you will be able to not only know God's will, but also be able to prove it.

Through fasting and prayer we possess the ability to change not only ourselves, but the outcome of our situations.

Are you ready for a change?

I AM A 100% TITHER...

- Because I am obedient to God's Word, I reap the benefits of God. The windows of Heaven are open unto me.

- Blessings are poured out upon me, the devourer is rebuked from me, and the fruits of my hands shall last and not be destroyed.

- All the people call me "blessed" because I am a 100% Tither.

- I give unto God's kingdom and the windows of Heaven are open unto me.

- Because I am a 100% Tither, I am the head and not the tail.

- Because I am a 100% Tither, I am above and not beneath.

- Because I am 100% Tither, I am the lender and not the borrower.

- Praise God because I am a 100% TITHER!

ARE YOU BEING A GOOD STEWARD?
God said the Nation has robbed Him...
In the Bible there were two kinds of treasurers or stewards
- the good steward like the Ethiopian enoch who was entrusted with the treasures of the queen (Acts 8:27) or...
- the bad steward like Judas Iscariot... (John 12:6)

We have to keep the books. As good stewards, all of us are treasurers and entrusted with God's money.

Are we holding back part of God's money like Judas, or can we be trusted like the Ethiopian eunuch?

WHERE DOES THE TITHE GO?

Now that the tithe is collected, where does it go, and what is it used for? This question is rarely answered, but there is a good reason for the collecting of the tithe. God designed the practice of tithing to further His kingdom in more ways than one. True, it is to help support the preaching of the Gospel around the world by way of television, radio, internet, missionaries, evangelism, or purchasing materials to send around the world. God's tithe is used for much more than just that. Let's look closely to a few scriptures to see just how the Holy Tithe was distributed.

The tithe is used for the need of people;

Acts 4:34-37

For the Priest and the Levites (Ministers of the Lord)

Lev.2:3, Lev. 7:7-9, Dt. 18:3, 2 Ki. 12:16, 2 Chron. 31:2-11

What if I borrow the tithe, what do I need to repay?

If you borrow the tithe, the Bible instructs us to pay an additional 20% on the money we have borrowed. Example, you used $10.00 of your tithe, you would pay back the $10.00 and an additional $2.00 totaling $12.00. Lev. 27:31 says, *And if a man will at all redeem ought of his tithes, he shall add thereto the fifth part thereof.*

SAMPLE CHURCH INCOME STATEMENT
(with 300 members)

Ordinary Income/Expenses

Income

Building Fund	$6,406
Tithes/Offerings	$248,974
Total Income	**$255,380**

Expenses

Automobile		$1,798
Bank Service Charges		196
Computer/Internet		600
Contract Labor		1,080
Donations		4,210
Dues/Subscriptions		2,230
Equipment Rental		9,000
Flowers & Gifts		909
Insurance		
Medical	6,030	
Other Insurance	1,544	
Total Insurance Expenses		7,574
Laundry/Dry Cleaning		3,105
Benevolence/Needy Families		4,031
Payroll		
Payroll Gross		13,725

Housing Allowance	2,700	
Other Payroll Expenses	28,575	
Total Payroll Expenses		45,000
Professional Fees		
Accounting	1,150	
Honorariums	8,388	
Other Professional Fees	380	
Total Professional Fees		9,918
Rent Expense		36,000
Repairs & Maintenance		
Building/Property Security	1,185	
Landscaping	1,861	
Other Repairs/Maintenance	11,244	
Total Repairs/Maintenance		14,290
Supplies		
Church	75,479	
Office	1,581	
Total Supplies		77,060
Telephone Expenses		1,900
Utilities		3,185
Outreach Expenses		2,700
Food Bank		3,000
Missionary Expenses		5,343
Total Expenses		**$233,129**
Net Income		**$22,251**

The Firstfruits is a spiritual law that was established before the law of Moses in the Old Testament. Tithing was practiced from the beginning with Cain and Abel, and then through Abraham, which was 430 years before the law was given; and was later made part of the law of Moses. Tithing was also practiced by the churches under the grace of the New Testament.

Genesis 4:4	Lev. 27:30	Matt. 17:24-27
Genesis 14:20	Num. 18:21-24	Matt. 22:21
Genesis 28:22	Deut. 14:27-29	Matt. 23:23
Hebrews 7:1-11	Malachi 3:10	Mark 12:41
		Luke 11:42
		Luke 12:42-44
		Luke 18:11-12

A DIVINE LAW

430 Years Before the Law | **Part of the Law** | **New Testament Grace**

THE FIRST FRUITS

Now that you have heard this Word about the firstfruits, I want to remind you that the Bible teaches, "Be doers of the word, and not hearers only, deceiving your own selves." [James 1:22]

If the principles taught in this book have come alive in your heart, I ask you NOW to put your faith into action by sowing a seed into Whole Man Ministries.

I have placed an image of my hand here to symbolize the power of agreement. Jesus said, "That if two of you shall agree on earth as touching any thing that they shall ask, it shall be done for them of my Father which is in heaven." [Matthew 18:19]

I want to agree with you that the seed you sow into Whole Man Ministries will produce a hundredfold return in Jesus's name. Amen.

Send your seed in FAITH to:

Whole Man Ministries
3916 Old Lexington Road
Winston-Salem NC 27107

Brief Telephone Continuing Care Therapy for Adolescents

Brief Telephone Continuing Care Therapy for Adolescents

Yifrah Kaminer, M.D., M.B.A.
Chris Napolitano, M.S., L.M.F.T.

HAZELDEN®

Hazelden
Center City, Minnesota 55012
hazelden.org

© 2010 by Hazelden Foundation
All rights reserved. Published 2010
Printed in the United States of America

The material on the CD-ROM may be duplicated for personal or group use. Otherwise, no part of this publication may be reproduced, stored in a retrieval system, or transmitted in any form or by any means—electronic, mechanical, photocopying, recording, scanning, or otherwise—without the express written permission of the publisher. Failure to comply with these terms may expose you to legal action and damages for copyright infringement.

ISBN: 978-1-59285-477-6

Editor's note
The names, details, and circumstances may have been changed to protect the privacy of those mentioned in this publication.

This publication is not intended as a substitute for the advice of health care professionals.

Cover and interior design by David Farr, ImageSmythe
Typesetting by David Farr, ImageSmythe

Hazelden, a national nonprofit organization founded in 1949, helps people reclaim their lives from the disease of addiction. Built on decades of knowledge and experience, Hazelden offers a comprehensive approach to addiction that addresses the full range of patient, family, and professional needs, including treatment and continuing care for youth and adults, research, higher learning, public education and advocacy, and publishing.

A life of recovery is lived "one day at a time." Hazelden publications, both educational and inspirational, support and strengthen lifelong recovery. In 1954, Hazelden published *Twenty-Four Hours a Day,* the first daily meditation book for recovering alcoholics, and Hazelden continues to publish works to inspire and guide individuals in treatment and recovery, and their loved ones. Professionals who work to prevent and treat addiction also turn to Hazelden for evidence-based curricula, informational materials, and videos for use in schools, treatment programs, and correctional programs.

Through published works, Hazelden extends the reach of hope, encouragement, help, and support to individuals, families, and communities affected by addiction and related issues.

For questions about Hazelden publications, please call **800-328-9000** or visit us online at **hazelden.org/bookstore.**

Contents

Acknowledgments vii

Introduction 1

Part 1 Essential Ingredients

Chapter 1 The Program at a Glance 5
Chapter 2 Session Structure 13
Chapter 3 Setting Up the Program 19
Chapter 4 Troubleshooting 25

Part 2 Clinician's Guide

Session 1 Assessing Client Needs, Establishing Goals, and Reviewing Coping Skills 33
Sessions 2 through 5 39

Appendixes

Appendix 1 How the Program Works: A Case Vignette 53
Appendix 2 Progression of Sessions 55
Appendix 3 The Five Main MET Strategies 75
Appendix 4 Additional MET Guidelines 77

References 79
About the Authors 83

v

Acknowledgments

THE DEVELOPMENT OF THIS MANUAL followed the evolution of theory-driven protocols for the treatment of adult and adolescent alcohol and substance abuse. The adult-based literature includes cognitive behavioral therapy CBT (Monti et al. 1989) and brief motivational interviewing (MI), known also as Motivational Enhancement Therapy (MET) (Kadden et al. 1992), which was developed while considering the influential transtheoretical paradigm of change (Prochaska, DiClemente, and Norcross 1992) and Miller and Rollnick's (2002) seminal work on MI. The adolescent literature included two MET/CBT manuals developed at our Alcohol Research Center at the University of Connecticut Health Center for the multicenter Cannabis Youth Treatment (CYT) study (Sampl and Kadden 2001; Webb et al. 2002).

The authors also wish to graciously acknowledge the following contributors to the development of the first draft of the Brief Individual Aftercare Therapy Algorithm: Dr. James McKay of the University of Pennsylvania and Dr. Susan Sampl of the University of Connecticut Health Center.

Introduction

THIS THERAPY PROGRAM ADDRESSES THE NEED for reliable, brief, and cost-effective aftercare for adolescents with alcohol and other substance use disorders (AOSUD). Its aim is to establish a viable alternative method for delivering high-quality intervention via the brief telephone intervention when significant impediments in distance, weather, transportation, staffing, space, funding, and other resources may limit the delivery of traditional face-to-face therapeutic contact. Nevertheless, the program may also be used in a traditional face-to-face psychotherapy session because the active ingredients are similar. The only difference is that the clinician will have fewer nonverbal cues to help facilitate dialogue.

The telephone as a readily accessible interpersonal medium has a variety of therapeutic uses (Rutter 1987). Its use in crisis intervention (Spirito et al. 2002), advice provision, and after-hours triage is common among adolescents and their caregivers (Baker et al. 1999; Kaminer 1994). According to studies of alcoholic clients who have completed treatment, communication between client and clinician via telephone has played an increasing role in the therapeutic process since the 1960s (Catanzaro and Green 1970; Intagliata 1976; Koumans, Muller, and Miller 1967).

This clinician's manual includes the essential components of the program and specific instructions on how to implement it. These include the models of change and psychotherapy that are integrated into the approach, the goals and objectives, the potential settings that the program might be used in, the types of clients appropriate for receiving the intervention, the rationale for its use, and the clinical and evaluation/supervision issues.

The manual also includes a clinician's guide that provides step-by-step instructions for each session. Examples of dialogue that a clinician might employ during the course of a session are provided.

Part 1
Essential Ingredients

Chapter 1
The Program at a Glance

THE BRIEF TELEPHONE THERAPY PROGRAM is designed to deliver a treatment regimen of continuing care for adolescents and young adults who have a mild to moderate substance use disorder and have recently completed a more intensive course of treatment. The program is brief both in the number of sessions (five) and the time required to deliver the sessions. It is designed to be implemented over a twelve-week period. The first session is a fifty-minute office session, while the remaining four sessions should take approximately fifteen minutes each. Ideally, session 1 should occur within two weeks of the completion of the more intensive AOSUD treatment phase. Sessions 2 and 3 are delivered two weeks following session 1 (and are also two weeks apart). Sessions 4 and 5 are delivered three weeks after session 3 (and are also three weeks apart).

What Treatment Models Does the Program Use?

The program combines components of MI/MET and CBT into an algorithm (see the diagram on page 16) that is based on the client's present level of substance use and the degree of motivation to achieve desired goals (Kaminer and Napolitano 2004). This formula was derived in part on the notion that if a particular individual is sufficiently motivated to achieve his own identified goals, then the focus of the session can be *how* to help the client achieve those goals using CBT coping skills, by targeting high-risk situations. Within the

CBT framework, the process includes an emphasis on coping skills that may be useful and/or necessary for the individual to incorporate, or continue using, in his life to help achieve desired goals. According to the algorithm, an identified level of intrinsic motivation must be present for the session to proceed to a CBT dialogue about the use of coping strategies in high-risk situations. If the client's motivation for change is not sufficient, the session then targets this aspect with the use of MI/MET. The client's goals are defined with the help of the clinician in the first aftercare session.

The treatment algorithm that guides the flow of dialogue between clinician and client is based in part on the stages of change theory proposed by Prochaska, DiClemente, and Norcross (1992). The stages of change theory proposes that an individual progresses through a predictable process of internal reflection as she considers the idea of change. Motivational interviewing/enhancement strategies in this substance abuse aftercare intervention aim to facilitate this naturally occurring process. By meeting clients at the stage of change they are in relative to the behavior of substance abuse, clinicians can simultaneously enhance clients' motivation to continue moving forward in the stages of change framework. The clinician uses dialogue focused on reducing resistance, emphasizing the client's stated reasons for change, focusing on a future-oriented mindset, and other strategic language that is designed to increase the client's motivation for change.

When clients are deemed to have a "sufficient" degree of motivation to change (to be discussed in detail later), CBT coping skills strategies become the primary emphasis of the session. Coping skills are designed to address internal and external factors that present "high-risk" circumstances—that is, predictors that increase the likelihood that substance use will occur. Those particular aspects, while highly specific to each individual, will generally fall into the category of "internal triggers" or "external triggers." Internal triggers are factors that occur inside an individual (intrapersonally), such as thoughts, emotions, moods, cravings, and urges. External triggers are factors that occur in the individual's context (interpersonally), such as relationships with friends and family, exposure to drugs and alcohol, and peer pressure (Marlatt 1996). Often, there is a dynamic relationship between internal and external triggers. For example, an individual may have a conflict with a family member (external trigger) that results in feeling angry and depressed (internal triggers). The combination of these factors can increase the degree to which an individual experiences craving or has an urge (internal triggers) to use a particular substance. Cognitive-behavioral coping skills aim to help the individual use a productive/adaptive means of coping with these internal and external factors so that the individual has a variety of other more productive options readily available to cope with high-risk situations, thereby decreasing the likelihood that alcohol or drug use will occur (Kadden et al. 1992).

As clients experience success by employing these more adaptive/productive skills, their self-efficacy—that is, confidence in their ability to refrain from substance use in high-risk situations—increases. Increase in self-efficacy is correlated with increased abstinence rates (Burleson and Kaminer 2005). Emphasis on reducing the negative consequences of substance use, and increasing the positive benefits of change, is part of the interplay between MET and CBT. The clinician acts as an empathic mentor, teacher, and guide in the learning process and implementation of productive coping skills for high-risk situations.

Is the Program Evidence Based?

The Adolescent Alcohol Treatment and Outcome Maintenance (AATOM) study was conducted at the University of Connecticut Health Center, Department of Psychiatry, from 2001 to 2006 by Dr. Yifrah Kaminer. The study investigated the effects of an aftercare intervention for adolescents ages thirteen to eighteen, treated initially for AOSUD with nine weekly group sessions of CBT. This treatment phase was followed by a twelve-week aftercare regimen similar to the aftercare process described in this manual. Following the nine sessions of CBT group therapy, subjects were randomly assigned to one of the following conditions:

- five fifty-minute sessions of in-person aftercare
- one session of individual therapy followed by four fifteen-minute aftercare sessions via the telephone
- no active aftercare

Results from this study indicated that, first, the phone intervention is feasible and acceptable for both adolescents and clinicians (Burleson and Kaminer 2007). Second, the twelve-week aftercare treatment phase following an initial course of nine weekly CBT group therapy sessions was significantly better than the "no aftercare" treatment condition. Further, there was no statistically significant difference between subjects assigned to the five individual in-person aftercare sessions and the subjects assigned to the telephone aftercare sessions (Kaminer, Burleson, and Burke 2008). These results were maintained during a nine-month follow-up, although the magnitude of difference gradually decreased (Burleson, Kaminer, and Burke 2009). In conclusion, aftercare interventions for substance use disorders in adolescents can help maintain progress made by individuals in an initial treatment phase. The results also indicate that the telephone is at least as effective a modality as in-person sessions for delivery of aftercare.

It is also noteworthy that aftercare interventions reduced suicidal ideations compared to the "no active intervention" condition (Kaminer et al. 2006).

What Are the Program's Goals and Objectives?

In terms of substance use, the goals of the program are client driven. Let's say, for example, that an individual had been using a particular substance (such as alcohol or marijuana) heavily in terms of frequency and/or quantity, but was able to reduce her use significantly during the more intensive phase of treatment. The client would now like to maintain a level of use that is less harmful, but is not motivated for abstinence. In session 1, the clinician would help the individual define a goal with specific parameters for her substance use based on this agenda. During this dialogue, the clinician can use MET language to help emphasize to the client her own reasons for change. A discussion of abstinence and how the individual feels about the idea can be useful, but caution should be used to avoid pressuring an agenda the clinician may have for the client in this direction. The goal for the clinician is to avoid eliciting resistance while staying just ahead of where the client is in her own thought process, and/or stage of change, in relation to substance use.

Other goals that are set during the first session should also be client driven. With the guidance of the clinician, specific goals can be identified that are (1) related in some way to the client's substance use and (2) deemed to be productive for the client. For example, the individual may have a goal of using alcohol only once per month, but struggles to think of what other activities could be incorporated that would be fun and exciting. The clinician might suggest that a goal be to establish new activities for fun and excitement. A dialogue could then ensue on how to go about doing this. Other goals can be set in a similar fashion.

Why Use Brief Individual Aftercare Therapy with Drug-Abusing Youth?

Kaminer, Burleson, and Burke (2008) describe three potential short-term treatment outcomes for adolescents diagnosed with AOSUD:

1. reaching the most desired objective, abstinence
2. achieving partial improvement, such as reduction in symptom count and severity of use (for example, frequency, dosage, type of drug(s) used, and consequences)
3. no response to treatment

Although improvement is obtained in treatment by a significant number of youth, the pathway to adulthood rarely includes abstinence. Treatment is usually followed by relapse rates of more than 60 percent three to twelve months after treatment completion (Brown, Vik, and Creamer 1989; Kaminer, Burleson, and Goldberger 2002). These findings do not come as a surprise given the growing consensus that AOSUD is a chronic, relapsing, and remitting disorder characterized by periods of abstinence followed by relapse (McLellan et al. 2000; O'Brien and McLellan 1996) and reentry into the treatment system (McKay et al. 2004). Hence, there is a need to increase the overall effectiveness of treatment as well as maintain treatment gains by developing and testing the efficacy of behavioral aftercare interventions and services for youths.

There has not been a clear consensus regarding what terms should be used to describe post-treatment interventions. Partially overlapping terms—such as "continued care," "aftercare," "step-down," or "transition of care"—have been used interchangeably.

The American Society of Addiction Medicine (2001) has defined continued care as "the provision of a treatment plan and organizational structure that will ensure that a patient receives whatever kind of care necessary at the time. Thus the program is flexible and tailored to the shifting needs of the patient's level of readiness to change."

Lack of continuity of care or aftercare programs for adults (McKay 1999) and adolescents with AOSUD is the rule rather than the exception (Kaminer 2001). The only aftercare intervention with youth successfully tested so far has been the Assertive Community Reinforcement Approach (Godley et al. 2007).

In addition to providing flexibility by using the telephone for treatment delivery, this program can benefit youth through several means. Since the client directs the variables for producing positive change, there is likely to be less resistance experienced by both the clinician and the client. Essentially, the clinician asks the client in the first session, "Where are you right now in relation to drug and alcohol use, and what do you want to accomplish from here?" Given that the expectation for the clinician is to refrain from projecting his ideas for change onto the client, clients are then freer to say what they believe to be most useful to achieve their treatment goal. This process helps support the self-efficacy of the client, which is an important aspect related to positive outcome in substance use disorders (Annis et al. 1989).

Additionally, this process helps increase the therapeutic alliance between the client and clinician, which is also a significant predictor of positive treatment outcome (Duncan, Miller, and Sparks 2004). The clinician provides a framework and focuses attention on the client's ideas about how to continue improving (what coping skills to work on, what goals to set, and so on). Even if/when resistance is elicited or experienced in a session, clinicians rely on MET strategies that are aimed at eliciting and maintaining motivation to change substance abuse. This approach is consistent with the developmental stage of adolescence in that this age group is more likely to respond to a "what's in it for me, what do I want" process, which can fuel motivation. Motivation then fuels effort, and effort fuels self-efficacy and outcome, which then reinforce this positive cycle to continue.

Why Use the Telephone to Conduct This Therapy?

Recent reports have supported the effectiveness of telephone-based continued care in the clinical management of clients with AOSUD (Breslin et al. 1996; McKay et al. 2004). Zhu et al. (1996) demonstrated the effectiveness of using the telephone as a means of providing therapeutic support for smoking cessation.

Gumpert and Fish (1990) reported that in many cases the telephone was the client's preferred means of communication with the clinician due to its ability to bridge distance and transportation problems, appointment conflicts, and contact boundaries (for example, phone contact may encourage disclosure by minimizing the perception of risk and vulnerability). The phone contact is essentially a two-way and relatively private communication. Thus, interpersonal relationships may be successfully developed and/or maintained over the telephone and improve compliance with follow-up procedures (Intagliata 1976; Williams 1984).

Which Clients Can Benefit from Brief Telephone Therapy?

This program is most likely to help produce positive change in youths ages thirteen to eighteen who have completed a prior course of AOSUD treatment. Clients need not be completely abstinent from drugs and alcohol to participate in this program. They may be youths who are deemed at risk for continued substance abuse, or those who made only small changes in their previous treatment episode. Individuals who are still using alcohol or drugs more frequently may be considered for this program on a case-by-case basis; however, a clinical determination will need to be made to decide whether this intervention will be sufficient or if a more intensive course of treatment is indicated.

Who Can Implement the Program?

This method of providing brief AOSUD management in aftercare is designed for a trained behavioral health specialist who may use it to deliver, monitor, or enhance treatment and aftercare of a given case. Behavioral health specialists may include specifically trained psychiatrists, counselors, marital and family therapists, psychologists, and social workers. With proper training and supervision, professionals working in the criminal justice system (such as probation officers) and school psychologists might also be able to implement the program.

How Can You Evaluate the Effectiveness of This Aftercare Intervention?

Ideally, clinicians who are trained in conducting this intervention are routinely supervised to ensure that aspects of the program are being implemented according to manual guidelines. Whether aftercare sessions 2 through 5 are conducted by telephone or completed in person, they can be audiotaped with the client's consent, and these tapes can be rated using the Brief Telephone Therapy Supervision Rating Form (on the CD-ROM). Since there are very few differences in conducting the intervention in person or via telephone, the supervision rating form can be used to rate the clinician for both interventions. Informed consent for audiotaping is included in the Client Contract for Aftercare (on the CD-ROM).

If regular supervision of clinicians is not possible, self-review and ratings of audiotaped sessions will be helpful in ensuring that essential components of the intervention are being employed consistently.

Chapter 2

Session Structure

THIS AFTERCARE INTERVENTION IS UNIQUE because the therapy can be delivered via the telephone, but it can also be used in traditional face-to-face psychotherapy. There are five sessions in this program. The first session is fifty minutes in length and should be conducted in person. The remaining four sessions take approximately fifteen minutes each to conduct.

> A note about session length: In the AATOM study, fifteen-minute telephone aftercare sessions were adhered to for research protocol purposes. Clinicians employing the aftercare intervention using this manual may not be required to adhere to the research protocol time period; however, it should be noted that results from the study are based on performing the telephone intervention using a fifteen-minute time block.

Ideally, session 1 should occur within two weeks of the completion of the more intensive AOSUD treatment. Sessions 2 and 3 are delivered two weeks following the previous session and are two weeks apart, with sessions 4 and 5 being delivered three weeks from the previous session, also being three weeks apart.

Components of Session 1

Various interventions are employed by the clinician in the first session that set the general agenda for the following four sessions. Included in the first session are the following components:

- a review of substance use past and present, and clinical issues that may need attention during aftercare
- a measure of motivation at the present time in relation to substance use
- an exploration of potential high-risk situations (both internal and external factors) that characterize each client
- a review of coping skills that can be incorporated into sessions 2 through 5

Clinicians also help the client formulate and set goals in the first session. The Client Summary Sheet for Aftercare (CSSA) and the Goal-Setting Worksheet are the forms that are used for these processes. These forms, as well as detailed instructions on how to use them, are included on the CD-ROM.

In-Person versus Telephone Format for Sessions 2 through 5

Offering the program in whole or in part as a telephone intervention increases the degree of flexibility for treatment delivery (eliminating issues surrounding transportation or distance to clinics, weather, and office space, and offering more flexibility in scheduling appointments). In many circumstances, this is a more feasible and acceptable option to clients and clinicians alike (Kaminer and Napolitano 2004; Burleson and Kaminer 2007). These factors have the potential to increase the percentage of individuals who remain engaged in the aftercare treatment process.

Whether the intervention is delivered via telephone or in person, there is little difference in the process. Sessions 2 through 5 follow the same three-part algorithm. One difference between telephone contacts and in-person contacts is the need to check for appropriate privacy during the phone calls. The clinician will also need to make adjustments due to the fact that he will not be able to pick up on all of the client's nonverbal cues. Therefore, it may be helpful to listen more carefully, pay close attention to the tone and manner behind the client's words, ask for clarification whenever necessary, and compliment statements of self-efficacy.

Using the Algorithm

The goals of session 1 are to build rapport, gather information, review progress, and set agendas. Sessions 2 through 5 are considered the intervention sessions, during which specific therapeutic strategies focused on helping the client achieve desired goals are employed by the clinician. The three-part algorithm helps simplify this complex process (see the "Brief Individual Aftercare Therapy Algorithm" on page 16).

STEP 1 ▸▸▸
Establish rapport.

The first steps of the algorithm allow for joining or building rapport with the client, while addressing her present level of substance use and level of motivation related to substance use. The following steps focus on the delivery of specific therapeutic interventions based on those factors.

STEP 2 ▸▸▸
Review substance use and establish level of motivation.

The clinician inquires about the present level of substance use. Generally speaking, one of three responses can be expected to the question "How have things been going for you in terms of substance use?" The possible responses by the client will be one of the following:

1. complete abstinence
2. a reduction in substance use
3. a level of substance use that is similar to or greater than that reported in the first aftercare session

Brief Individual Aftercare Therapy Algorithm

Step 1 Briefly establish or reestablish rapport.

Step 2 Assess current level of use. Use step 2A, 2B, or 2C as indicated.

Step 2A Client reports NO SUBSTANCE USE since last contact.

- Reinforce and congratulate for abstinence/progress.
- Identify and reinforce coping skills that have been working using the Coping Skills Summary Sheet.
- Probe for any upcoming potential high-risk situations.
- Briefly discuss plan of action until the next session.

Step 2B Client reports using since last contact and is ADEQUATELY MOTIVATED for change (motivation rated 5 or above).

- Use CSSA and/or Aftercare Post-Session Summary Sheet to address problem areas.
- Review coping skills as needed using the Coping Skills Summary Sheet.
- Reinforce any and all attempts and/or willingness to apply these skills.
- Combine with MET language and interventions if motivation for change is questionable.

Step 2C Client reports using since last contact and is NOT ADEQUATELY MOTIVATED for change (motivation rated below 5).

- Use MI/MET techniques only to address motivation and readiness to change factors.

*NOTE: If substance use has become severe, consider referring for more intensive treatment; discuss treatment alternatives with client. Discuss case with supervisor, if necessary.

Steps 3A and 3B Close the call following CBT intervention, or CBT plus MET intervention.

- Summarize the main points; reiterate direct suggestions of coping skills to develop or enhance.
- Give generous positive feedback about the client's participation in the call.
- Schedule the next session.

Step 3C Close the call following MET intervention.

- Summarize the discussion and make a motivational statement of hope for change regarding motivation to achieve abstinence or work toward change.
- Give generous positive feedback about the client's participation in the call.
- Schedule the next session.

If the client responds by affirming abstinence, the clinician inquires as to the level of motivation present to continue to maintain abstinence on a 0–10 scale, with 0 being not at all motivated and 10 being extremely motivated.

Scaling Client Motivation to Change

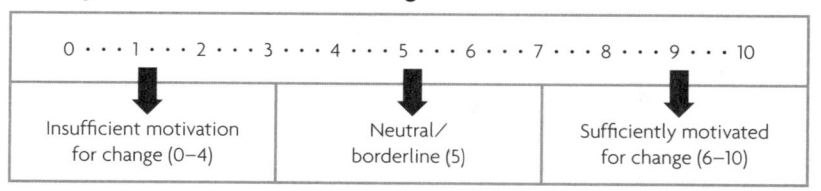

0 ··· 1 ··· 2 ··· 3 ··· 4 ··· 5 ··· 6 ··· 7 ··· 8 ··· 9 ··· 10
Insufficient motivation for change (0–4)   Neutral/borderline (5)   Sufficiently motivated for change (6–10)

A rating of 5 or above is the cue for the clinician to proceed to a CBT coping skills dialogue, that is, to discuss what kinds of thoughts and behaviors (skills) the individual has been incorporating into his life that have helped maintain abstinence. During this discussion, the clinician refers to information in the CSSA that was filled out with the client in session 1 and the Coping Skills Summary Sheet (on the CD-ROM) as guides for the dialogue.

If the client reports some level of substance use since the last session, the clinician inquires as to the level of motivation to change in order to make a decision on how to proceed with the dialogue. Motivation to maintain or work toward abstinence is used as a guide for facilitating the dialogue further. Again, a rating of 5 or above is an indicator that the client is sufficiently motivated to move toward a focus on CBT coping skills. In other words, clients who are sufficiently motivated guide the clinician toward a discussion of coping skills relevant to the individual, while those who are not adequately motivated guide the clinician toward the use of MET to help target readiness for change. The guiding principle is that if clients are lacking in intrinsic motivation to apply coping skills, it doesn't make therapeutic sense to focus on coping skills that may be useful as an intervention to produce change.

There may be cases where self-efficacy plays a role in motivation. If, for example, a client feels that he doesn't have the ability to be successful (that is, to remain sober in high-risk situations), there is likely to be less motivation to make attempts. To help support self-efficacy, the clinician can acknowledge past efforts or encourage the client to experience just how positive being successful during a high-risk situation can feel. The algorithm is intended to provide an overall structure and framework for each session, while accounting for a portion of these individual complexities. In cases where

Session Structure **17**

motivation is questionable or borderline, which is usually indicated by a rating of 5 on the 0–10 scale, it will be the judgment of the clinician whether to emphasize MET strategies, coping skills dialogue, or a combination of both approaches.

> **NOTE:** If at any time during this program the client seems to have returned to a more intensive level of substance use, an open dialogue should ensue to discuss options for a return to more intensive treatment.

Coping skills that are emphasized in the session will depend on information that was gathered in session 1 as well as present reports from the client. This process will be discussed in further detail later in the guide.

STEP 3 ▸▸▸
Close the session.

The final part of the algorithm is closing the session. This is a brief summary of the session, with the clinician giving generous praise and positive feedback about the client's participation in the session. Plans for the next session are also made at this time.

Chapter 3

Setting Up the Program

SINCE THIS PROGRAM IS BRIEF and incorporates the use of the telephone, it can be used in a number of different settings by a variety of professionals.

Clinical Settings

Clinics are ideal settings to establish this aftercare intervention program. Clients can be referred to aftercare seamlessly following a course of group or individual AOSUD treatment. Staff should introduce the merit of participating in an aftercare intervention during an individual's treatment phase. Clients can be briefed on the characteristics and benefits of the program and ask questions. The idea of the intervention being employed via the telephone can make participation more palatable for those clients who resist further in-person treatment contacts.

A procedure can be established by any agency to implement this aftercare program. The steps might include the following:

- Establish policies and procedures to include aftercare as a routine component for adolescent AOSUD treatment. Train staff in the implementation of the aftercare program.
- Identify clients deemed appropriate for five sessions of aftercare. Consider the client's degree of severity of use near the end of AOSUD treatment. Either mild to moderate severity of substance use or complete abstinence are

considered appropriate criteria for acceptance into this aftercare program.

- Brief the identified clients on the program prior to finishing more intensive treatment.
- Process informed consent with parents.
- Schedule session 1 of aftercare two weeks following the client's final treatment session.

Use of This Program in Nontraditional Treatment Settings

It may be feasible that this aftercare program can be utilized in settings other than traditional clinic treatment centers. Examples might be clinical day school settings, public school settings, or juvenile detention centers. Care should be taken when establishing policies and procedures within these alternative treatment milieus to safeguard for confidentiality, liability, and other factors that may be considered for appropriate mental health treatment. While some of these components are processed below, the scope of this manual is limited to a general discussion of these issues and should not be considered as a template for the establishment of treatment in alternative settings.

Create working alliances.

Setting up this aftercare program in an alternative school setting, juvenile detention center, or public school system could be achieved with collaboration from existing treatment facilities and/or behavioral service providers. Working alliances with community substance abuse treatment programs could be established to promote aftercare in the school system in order to maintain gains made by the client during the treatment phase. School administration, program directors and other administrative staff, and boards of education would need to be willing to consider the idea of providing AOSUD aftercare treatment contacts as part of policies and procedures.

Since youth spend many hours a day in these settings, they provide a convenient location to establish a brief AOSUD aftercare program.

The Transition to Aftercare Form (on the CD-ROM) can be used to help these systems in facilitating transition of clients from treatment to the aftercare treatment program. Release of information and parental consent forms will also need to be signed by the client's parents/guardians. More details on establishing the program in alternative settings are offered below.

Block out time for sessions.

Facilitating this aftercare program in alternative settings should require only minimal interruption in the youth's schedule. For session 1, a fifty-minute block of time will be required. Ideally, this session should occur during a study period or down time so that regular classroom time or other programming is not interfered with. In school settings, if it is decided that the student will miss classroom time to attend the first session, prior consent from parents/guardians and the client will be necessary (the CD-ROM contains a Parental Consent for Student to Participate in Aftercare Treatment on School Time). If the client has significant attendance issues and/or academic issues, these will need to be weighed when deciding whether to schedule sessions during class time.

If the telephone option is agreed on for a particular session, the session will need to be conducted after school has ended. Privacy is an important aspect for consideration when using the telephone as a therapeutic modality.

If the in-person method is chosen for a particular session, a fifteen- to thirty-minute block of time will be required. Again, ideally this should be arranged when an individual has free time, down time, or a study period. With parental and client consent, in-person sessions may occur during classroom time. Since there are only a total of five sessions over the course of twelve weeks, missing study period time and/or classroom time should not be considered a significant negative factor for administering the intervention. However, sessions should not be conducted on days when there is a test or a quiz occurring in a particular class.

Ensure privacy and confidentiality.

Confidentiality and privacy are important issues that need to be addressed when using this program in alternative settings. For example, if an individual's peers become aware that he is participating in a therapeutic intervention, that individual could become the target of ridicule, bullying, labeling/stereotyping, or other forms of embarrassment. This could potentially be a factor that would contribute to early termination of aftercare treatment.

Extreme caution should be used by clinicians to protect each client's privacy.

A school setting presents unique challenges in that clinicians are likely to see and potentially have contact with clients during a regular school day. Prior to instituting the program, procedures regarding confidentiality should be established by the school to prevent unforeseen circumstances. Even though a client might not be wary of his peers knowing about participation in the program at the outset, circumstances may develop that lead to negative outcomes for him. It is recommended that clinicians consider a "no acknowledgment" policy with youth who are participating in the program.

Other Settings

This program can also be used in criminal justice settings and in conjunction with other mental health treatment, affording clinicians and providers a brief, structured intervention to address substance use, in addition to other behavioral health issues being processed in counseling.

Consent Issues

Participation in psychosocial treatment by clients under the age of eighteen in most states requires parental consent. The Letter of Introduction and Parent/Guardian Consent Form (on the CD-ROM), sent by the treatment facility or individual provider, can introduce parents or guardians to the program. The letter details the curriculum of the treatment program and provides informed consent and confidentiality guidelines.

Transitioning Clients from Treatment to Aftercare

No more than a short description about the aftercare program and the client's participation needs to be communicated at the outset of treatment. Clients should be gently reminded about participating in the aftercare program about midway through their treatment phase, and then again shortly before treatment completion. This method will help clients get used to the idea that they'll still be in contact with a clinician who can help them with difficulties they may experience following treatment.

Individual providers and agencies should add an aftercare component routinely to AOSUD treatment for adolescents. The option of having contacts via telephone has the potential to make the program an attractive choice. Further, the brief length of the sessions might also increase clients' willingness to participate. General observations noted from adolescents' reactions in the AATOM study demonstrated a high degree of enthusiasm by clients for shortened sessions and telephone contacts.

Prepare the client.

It is not essential that the clinician of the aftercare intervention be the same person as the client's primary clinician in the initial treatment phase. There may be both advantages and disadvantages to clinician consistency or variability, mostly in terms of therapeutic alliance. If, for example, a client did not have a positive relationship with a primary treatment provider, a change to a new clinician may be welcomed. This factor might also be a negative in that a new therapeutic alliance will need to be formed if the provider is changed. The transition can be discussed briefly well in advance so that the client is informed whether there will be a change of clinician occurring with the onset of aftercare. This factor should, if possible, be determined early on in treatment and communicated to the client as soon as possible. If agencies or individuals do not know whether there will be a change in the provider of aftercare, it is better to inform the client that this is the case. The fewer surprises present about a client's participation in aftercare, the more likely it is that the therapeutic alliance will be stronger and resistance to aftercare intervention will be lower.

Since session 1 of this aftercare intervention is always conducted in person, it is not necessary for the clinician to meet with the client prior to beginning the program (assuming there is a change in providers). There is ample time to allow for joining and rapport building during the discourse in the first session. The Transition to Aftercare Form (TAF) can aid in the transition for clients who will be assigned to different providers (which will always be the case when the intervention is conducted within the school system).

Complete the appropriate sharing of client history.

The TAF is a brief worksheet that clinicians will fill out with general information regarding the client's history of substance use and clinical issues that may need attention during aftercare. This worksheet will be provided to clinicians prior to session 1 of aftercare. The clinician will use the form in the first session of aftercare to aid in the process of filling out the Client Summary Sheet for Aftercare (CSSA). A release of information form will need to be signed by the client, or a parent or guardian if the client is under the age of eighteen.

Chapter 4

Troubleshooting

CLINICIANS SHOULD BE AWARE of a variety of issues that could occur during the course of the therapy, including unavailability of a phone, change of a phone number, clients being difficult to reach, relapse, emotional crisis, sharing information with parents, parents' refusal to allow children to participate, and client dishonesty.

Handling Missed Calls and Client Unavailability

Arrangements for how therapeutic phone contacts will be scheduled and carried out are discussed with the client in the first in-person session of aftercare. Calls should be scheduled to occur at mutually convenient times; however, clinicians are responsible for making the calls to clients for scheduled sessions. If the client is not available to receive the clinician's call at the specified date and time, but someone answers the phone, the clinician should ask if it is known whether the client might be available soon. If it is known that the client will be available within a short time frame, if possible, the clinician should attempt another call in that period. If it is unknown when the client will be available, the clinician should ask if it is okay to try calling back in thirty minutes. In the event an answering machine is reached, clinicians may choose to leave a message that does not break confidentiality in any way, and then try calling back in thirty minutes. Any time a contact is made with someone other than the client, clinicians should identify themselves by name only, or ask to speak with the client's parent or guardian if necessary.

If after two tries the client cannot be reached, the clinician should attempt to reschedule the session at a later time, ideally no later than one week after the original appointment. As a general rule of thumb, attempts should be made to contact the clients at least once every twenty-four hours after the missed session. Should contact then be made, the clinician may choose to complete the session at that time if it is feasible, or the session may be rescheduled to be conducted as soon as possible.

Encouraging Client Participation While Managing Time during the Sessions

Sessions 2 through 5 will each take fifteen minutes to complete. Since time is limited, the session must be very focused and goal oriented. Clinicians will not have the luxury of allowing the client to expand on details of given situations, or to do so themselves. Therefore, the clinician must guide the call in the direction of pinpointing specific areas of strengths and weaknesses without sounding overtly abrupt with the client.

Clinicians should strive for a fifty-fifty ratio in terms of speaking and listening. Clinicians must convey a genuine interest in the client's well-being and current state of affairs during the opening part of the contact. Following this initial joining phase, the clinician will need to become more assertive in leading the direction of the session, while at the same time encouraging the client to actively participate in dialogue. The middle portion of the session is when the clinician can allow the conversation to become moderately in-depth. This process can be facilitated by balancing open-ended questions such as "We talked about this last time—what happens when you start getting down on yourself?" with closed-ended questions such as "Do you think you'd be willing to try thought stopping the next time you catch yourself thinking that way?" as well as balancing feedback with listening to responses:

> Feedback: **"Since you've really been struggling with your thoughts lately, I'm thinking that we should review the coping skill regarding how to handle negative thinking..."**
>
> Listening: **"Do you think that might help?"** ... *[Listen.]*

Ensuring Privacy and Confidentiality during a Telephone Session

Clinicians should ensure at the very beginning of telephone sessions that the client feels comfortable enough to talk openly during the call. Clients should be asked directly if they have an appropriate level of privacy to participate in the call given their current surroundings. If it appears that the client is in an awkward position and will not be able to fully participate, the clinician should consider asking whether or not the client would like to reschedule the session or if she can be reached at a different telephone number (such as a friend's house or pay phone), and do so if necessary.

Handling Inappropriate Language and/or Nonproductive Dialogue

Clients should not be allowed to use inappropriate language toward the clinician at any time during telephone contacts. If the client does use language that is not acceptable, the clinician should politely warn the client and ask him if he feels he can continue the call without talking in that manner. Clinicians should strive to set clear boundaries without communicating disrespect to the client. It may be useful for the clinician to attempt to briefly probe to find out the reason behind the behavior. For example, the client may have been arguing with a parent or friend just before the call.

Clinicians should make continual efforts to keep the dialogue of the phone call focused on issues pertaining to substance use and refrain from drifting away. It may be that there are times during the call when the client becomes less willing (resistant) to engage in dialogue around substance use. In these situations, the MI/MET strategy of "rolling with resistance" should be incorporated. For example, it may be that the client's motivation is low to make changes in her substance use behavior. The individual may not be saying very much in response to the clinician's dialogue. A typical MET strategy in this case would be to acknowledge the client's level of motivation and make gentle attempts to discuss negative consequences of continued use, while mentioning the brief fifteen-minute length of the call.

Handling Emergency Situations

Any issues that require immediate attention during a telephone session, such as threat of harm to self or others, should be handled in the same manner as they would be in face-to-face therapy—according to the guidelines at the clinician's respective clinic or individual practice. If the client is clearly under the influence of drugs or alcohol during the telephone session, do not continue to employ the phone intervention. Rather, before rescheduling and terminating the call, the clinician should explore safety concerns to the best of his ability, such as the potential for high-risk behavior (driving, swimming, illegal activity, plans to harm self or others, and so on). In this situation, it may be worthwhile to ask if someone else is available to talk to, such as a parent or guardian or friend, to ensure that the client is safe. If the client denies being under the influence although it is apparent that he may indeed have used recently, it will be the clinician's judgment whether to continue with the session.

Rescheduling Missed Telephone Sessions

Clinicians should be responsible for rescheduling telephone sessions that are missed because the client was not available at the time of the call. If the clinician is having difficulty reaching the client, a call to the client's locator will be necessary (see the Locator Form on the CD-ROM).

Arranging for an Alternative Venue

Some clients may not have an appropriate home environment for a therapeutic telephone contact. In the first in-person individual session, the clinician should discuss this issue to ensure that the client feels comfortable with the specified place for the call to occur. If it becomes clear that the home environment is not an appropriate location, the clinician should inquire if there is another location where the call could take place. Privacy and confidentiality should be stressed so that the therapeutic value of the call can be maximized. If no appropriate location can be determined, in some circumstances a phone card or cell phone may be supplied to the client so that she may phone the clinician. Calls should be scheduled in the same manner, on a specified date and time.

Addressing Client Relapse

If at any time the clinician suspects that the client has had a relapse—that is, a return to the same or to a more severe or sustained level of substance use—options for returning to more intensive treatment should be addressed and discussed openly. Clinicians should maintain a nonjudgmental stance toward clients at all times, regardless of their substance use. Dialogue should focus on relapse being a common part of recovery so that the client's self-efficacy is not further undermined through the discussion. If the clinician concludes that the client needs to receive a more intensive intervention, she should communicate this decision to the client. If clients are not willing to receive more intensive treatment, clinicians should make it clear that they cannot ethically continue to treat them with an intervention that is not designed to address more severe levels of substance use. A list of referrals should be given, and clients should be encouraged to use the clinicians to help arrange for more intensive treatment. Follow-up calls to resistant clients should be made within one week of the initial dialogue regarding the relapse to again offer assistance with arranging for more intensive treatment. Difficult cases should always be discussed with supervisors and documented well.

Sharing Information with Parents

With the exception of harm to self or others, clinicians should share information with parents or guardians regarding the client *only* if prior consent is given by the client to do so. In many cases, the client will have signed a release form during the initial treatment intake. In some cases, clear boundaries may need to be set with parents who contact clinicians intrusively to discuss their child's progress. Care should be taken in these cases to maintain a productive working alliance with the parents, while gently informing them that frequent contacts are not productive for the client's participation in aftercare treatment. Parents' attempts at overinvolvement can be reframed by the clinician as genuine care and concern for their child's well-being.

Parents and guardians have the potential to undermine the client's participation in treatment at any time. All questions about the program should be answered openly and in depth where necessary. Parents and guardians who are resistant to having their child participate in the program can be informed of the brief nature of the sessions, the option for sessions to be conducted via the telephone, and the evidence-based nature of aftercare treatment for adolescents with AOSUD. MI/MET strategies can be employed in dialogue, and additional joining and relationship building may be necessary at times to help get everyone on board and working in the same direction.

Encouraging Client Honesty/Ingenuity

Several aspects of this treatment program may help minimize the degree to which clients lie to their clinician about their substance use. Even though aftercare treatment goals are client centered—the use of MET strategies and the clinician's ongoing positive regard and empathy for the client are pivotal for treatment—there may still be times when clients, for one reason or another, are dishonest with clinicians. If the clinician suspects that this is the case, he may choose to address the issue directly with the client. Reassuring clients that their privacy is being protected and that they are free to be completely open is an option to consider. Gently expressing concern that if the client is withholding information, it will limit the degree to which he might be helped by the sessions is another. Clinicians may also reiterate that it is completely the client's choice to decide what he will take away from the sessions and that the clinician holds no judgment of him. Despite the clinician's best efforts, some clients will still not be honest. As long as there is no impending harm to self or others, in some cases there will not be anything more the clinician can do except to continue encouraging open dialogue and to employ MET strategies.

Part 2
Clinician's Guide

Session 1

Assessing Client Needs, Establishing Goals, and Reviewing Coping Skills

Goals

- Establish rapport. Review the Transition to Aftercare Form (TAF) from previous treatment.
- Complete Client Summary Sheet for Aftercare (CSSA) with client. Collaborate on specific topic areas to address in aftercare sessions.
- Collaborate on specific goals for client to work toward during twelve-week aftercare period.
- Review specific coping skills as indicated.
- Contract with client for next four aftercare sessions.

Time Required

60 minutes

Materials Needed

- Transition to Aftercare Form (TAF)
- Client Summary Sheet for Aftercare (CSSA)
- Goal-Setting Worksheet
- Coping Skills Summary Sheet
- Client Contract for Aftercare
- Aftercare Post-Session Summary Sheet

Preparation Needed

Review TAF prior to session.

The first in-person aftercare session is devoted to building rapport and setting the agenda for the next four aftercare sessions that will occur over the following twelve weeks. Clinicians should review the Transition to Aftercare Form (TAF) before the session.

STEP 1 ▸▸▸
Establish rapport and review client status.

Begin the session by briefly discussing factors that brought the client into treatment initially, what her life is like at the present time, and so on. For example, tell the client:

> Hi, _____. My name is _____. We're going to be working together over the next twelve weeks or so. I've taken a look at some information that was provided to me from your last treatment provider. I'd like to review this information with you now to make sure you agree with it.

Review the Transition to Aftercare Form (TAF) with the client at this point. Discuss how the client feels she has fared in the previous treatment, aspects regarding the sessions, coping skills that have helped, and in which areas the client would like to improve.

STEP 2 ▸▸▸
Complete the Client Summary Sheet for Aftercare (CSSA).

Next, complete the CSSA collaboratively with the client. There are four parts to the CSSA. Read through the instructions for each section of the form, and help the client derive answers. Tell the client:

> The next thing we're going to do together is fill in some information on this form—the CSSA—about where you feel you're at right now in relation to some issues that involve your substance use. We'll use the information on this form, and another one that we'll work on later, to guide some of what we'll be talking about in the upcoming sessions. Does that sound okay?

Identify client's level of motivation.

The first part of the form asks the client to identify her level of motivation at the present time in relation to substance use. In other words, if the client is abstinent, how motivated is he to continue being abstinent? If the client is using occasionally, how motivated is he to work toward reducing use? This helps the clinician gauge readiness for change, which, in part, will help guide the dialogue in this and future sessions (by either using more or less MET to facilitate motivation).

Identify the client's high-risk situations.

The second part of the CSSA is designed to help the client identify high-risk situations. The question to lead off with here is, "When are you most likely to use?" The clinician is trying to help determine under what circumstances the risk of using drugs and alcohol increases. It will be useful to give the client some examples, such as those listed on the CSSA form.

Rate the client's confidence.

The third part of the CSSA is "Situational Confidence" (Annis 1987). This is in part a continuation of the discussion about high-risk situations. The client is asked to rate to what degree she feels confident that substance use will not occur given the particular set of circumstances described in each example given. This will produce more information about the client's degree of self-efficacy and will target areas to focus on in the following sessions.

Be sure to make it clear that the *higher* the percentage rating is, the *higher* the degree of confidence present that substance use *will not* occur (and vice versa for lower percentage ratings). Note: Each individual may assign a different meaning to the percentage rating. In other words, 50 percent confidence to one client might reflect 75 percent to another client.

These ratings are designed to help give the clinician more information about the individual's self-efficacy and, generally speaking, to help the client become more aware of her own self-efficacy in specific circumstances. It is important to note that the client's own measure of self-efficacy should be considered as one component when helping her identify high-risk situations and appropriate coping skills to focus on in dialogue. The measure is not intended to be relied on in and of itself.

Identify coping skills.

The final part of the CSSA is to help identify particular coping skills that will be useful for the client to begin to incorporate or enhance, particularly in high-risk situations. For example, if an identified high-risk time for use is when the individual feels down or depressed, and the client has a low rating of confidence (low self-efficacy) in handling negative thoughts/emotions, it might be suggested that awareness and management of negative thinking be one coping skill to focus on. The client is also asked if there are other areas, in addition to the coping skills listed, that he feels it would be useful to spend some time focusing on in the following aftercare sessions. Those areas are then noted on the form.

STEP 3 ▸▸▸
Help the client identify goals.

The first goal listed on the Goal-Setting Worksheet will always be in relation to substance use. Clinicians should help clients shape goals to be realistic. Tell the client:

> **Great, now that we've identified some areas for us to focus on in our upcoming sessions, let's take a look at this next sheet. What we'll do here is have you come up with some ideas on where you'd like to be in the future—that is, things that you think you'd like to have happening in your life as you progress forward. We'll call them goals, but I prefer to think about them as aspects that *you* want to work at having become part of your reality for *you*, not for anyone else. The first aspect we'll identify is in relation to substance use. We've talked about your motivation in terms of substance use, so tell me what you think is a vision of how it will or won't be a factor for you here in the short term.**

A client's stated goal, for example, may be never to drink alcohol again. While the clinician can applaud the client for dedication to abstinence (and can encourage complete abstinence), she may also advise the client that in order to achieve this goal, a "one step at a time" approach will reduce the chances of failure. In this case, a shorter-term goal of staying abstinent during the next several weeks might be more realistic and achievable. Also, shorter-term goals are easier to reinforce, even if the client does not achieve them 100 percent. For example, if between sessions 1 and 2 of aftercare, the client has one episode of use when his stated goal was to be completely abstinent, the clinician can positively reinforce the client for achieving almost complete abstinence, as well as discuss the nature of the lapse. An important aspect is to help the client realize that achieving abstinence from alcohol and other drugs is a *process* and not an *event*.

Deflect resistance and develop discrepancy.

Engaging clients in a discussion of goals can sometimes evoke resistance, as clients may feel pressured to set an agenda they might not be willing to accept. Clinicians should use an empathic style and reflective listening to communicate an understanding of the difficulty involved in the process. Initially, clinicians should encourage clients to focus on what they would like to achieve, helping them form a personal vision of circumstances they would like to see manifest in their lives, rather than suggesting certain goals.

This may be facilitated in such a way as to develop areas of discrepancy between where the client currently is in the process and where he would prefer to be in an effort to elicit self-motivational statements for change (see "Develop Discrepancy" in Appendix 3: The Five Main MET Strategies, page 75). For example, a subject may state that she would like to be able to get along better with her parents (despite the fact that she continues to do things that elicit negative reactions from them). In an effort to help develop the discrepancy between her desire to get along better with her parents and her actual behaviors, the clinician could ask her how her current behaviors support that goal/vision for herself.

Some clients may struggle to think of specific goals other than limiting or eliminating substance use. Encouraging them to think of other goals that will help them achieve this can be helpful. For example, with a client who has few activities or hobbies apart from school, a goal could be to work on developing some new behaviors or take part in new activities that support an alcohol- or drug-free lifestyle. For this goal, a brief discussion could be focused on using the session materials "Increasing Pleasant Activities" on the Coping Skills Summary Sheet. In addition, possible avenues for achieving the goal (objectives) can be written to reinforce the idea that there are specific things the client can do (or think) that will be helpful. When it is completed, both the clinician and client should retain a copy of the Goal-Setting Worksheet for later reference.

STEP 4 ▶▶▶
Summarize and review coping skills that may be useful.

Based on the dialogue thus far, the clinician begins to summarize areas the client might benefit from focusing on in the following aftercare sessions. Tell the client:

Now that you've listed some ideas about what you'd like to have happen for yourself, let's take a closer look at some of the coping skills you checked off earlier on the first form. In terms of meeting the goal that you established for substance use, which of the tools or skills that we discussed might help you get there?

This summary should include an acknowledgment (without judgment) of the client's stated motivation, high-risk situations that are problematic, the client's self-efficacy, and specific coping skills the individual can consider applying during high-risk situations.

Give the client a copy of the Coping Skills Summary Sheet at this point, and a brief dialogue can ensue about a particular coping skill(s). During this discussion, the clinician should also be sure to ask what the client thinks a productive means of coping with a particular high-risk time/situation could be for herself to help support self-efficacy.

STEP 5 ▸▸▸
Review the Client Contract for Aftercare for the next four aftercare sessions. Schedule the next aftercare contact.

Using the Client Contract for Aftercare, explain the structure and format for the four aftercare sessions to follow. Review the date, time, and location for the next aftercare contact. If the contact will occur via telephone, be sure to emphasize to the client the importance of being available at the scheduled time and location of the call. Tell the client:

> **Great, so we just have a little more to do here today. Please read through this contract—it defines what we'll be doing over the next several weeks. Please note that there's a spot for you to initial indicating whether you are comfortable having our sessions audiotaped. With your permission, we do this only for the purpose of having a supervisor review our session to help me make sure that I've covered everything with you that I'm supposed to. Let me know if you have any questions.**

Sessions 2 through 5

Goals
- Establish rapport.
- Assess substance use and motivation.
- Use CBT coping skills dialogue, MI/MET, or a combination, depending on degree of motivation and whether substance use occurred since last contact.
- Close session; schedule next contact.

Time Required
Approximately 15 minutes

Materials Needed
- Transition to Aftercare Form (TAF)
- Client Summary Sheet for Aftercare (CSSA)
- Goal-Setting Worksheet
- Coping Skills Summary Sheet
- Client Contract for Aftercare (for contact information, if using phone)
- Aftercare Post-Session Summary Sheet from previous session, if applicable

Preparation Needed
Briefly review Aftercare Post-Session Summary Sheet, CSSA, and Goal-Setting Worksheet prior to session.

Aftercare sessions 2 through 5 are each conducted according to the three-step algorithm (see page 16). The process—that is, the specific steps that guide the dialogue—for each of these sessions remains the same.

STEP 1 ▸▸▸
Briefly reestablish rapport and summarize the purpose of the session.

Clinicians should begin the session by ensuring that the client has an appropriate level of privacy to continue (if the session is occurring by telephone), then briefly state the session's purpose and duration. For example, a telephone session might begin by stating the following:

> **Hi, Susan, this is Jackie from** [clinic name]**. Thanks for making yourself available today. We're only going be about fifteen minutes on the phone today, so let's get right to work. Do you have enough privacy to talk right now?** [Listen to response.] **How have you been doing since the last time we talked?**

In the first portion of the session, the clinician should begin by briefly talking with the client about how she is doing in general (asking what's been happening since the last session, how things have been going, and so on). This brief period of joining with the client should last no longer than a few minutes, during which the clinician is focused on engaging the client by demonstrating interest, understanding, and general concern for her current well-being. Clinicians should ensure that the client does not get overly involved in describing details of her life or current situations. Therefore, the client may need to be gently redirected to give a more general description of current functioning or events.

STEP 2 ▸▸▸
Assess current level of substance use and motivation for change.

This step of the session involves asking the client directly if there has been any substance use since the last contact, and if so, what type (alcohol or other drugs), how much, and how often. The clinician then mirrors back the response in a nonjudgmental fashion and follows by scaling the client's level of motivation. The following statement is an example of what clinicians might say during this step:

So, Susan, since the last time we talked, you've told me you used alcohol on one occasion, and you had about four drinks that day. Does that sound right? *[Listen for response. Then, in a neutral, nonjudgmental tone, say:]* **How motivated would you say you are at this point in time to either remain completely abstinent from alcohol or reduce your use?**

Scaling Client Motivation to Change

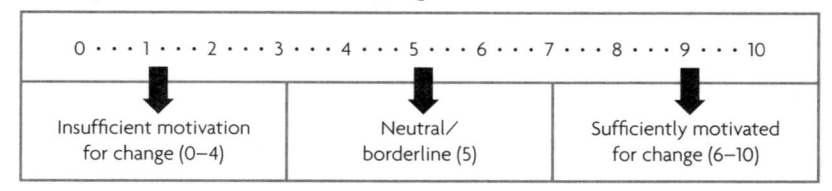

0 · · · 1 · · · 2 · · · 3 · · · 4 · · · 5 · · · 6 · · · 7 · · · 8 · · · 9 · · · 10
Insufficient motivation for change (0–4)   Neutral/ borderline (5)   Sufficiently motivated for change (6–10)

Depending on the client's level of substance use and motivation rating, the clinician then proceeds to one of the following steps:

- If no substance use is reported since the last contact, proceed to step 2A.
- If substance use is reported since the last contact, and motivation is rated at 5 or above, proceed to step 2B.
- If substance use is reported since the last contact, and motivation is rated at 4 or below, proceed to step 2C.

STEP 2A ▸▸▸
Client reports no substance use since last contact.

Reinforce abstinence with positive feedback; discuss coping strategies/methods of maintaining abstinence.

If the client reports abstinence since the last contact, ask how he feels about being abstinent and reinforce with positive feedback such as the following:

> **So you've been abstinent since our last meeting? That's really great! You must feel good about that.** *[Pause for response, allowing time for the client to express a sense of accomplishment.]*
>
> **Can you think of things that you've been doing or thinking about that have helped you remain abstinent? Have any of the coping skills that we previously discussed been helpful?**

The clinician may need to help the client identify specific coping skills that he may have used and found helpful. Reiterate and define the purpose and usefulness involved in using the given skill with the aid of the Coping Skills Summary Sheet. For example, if a client reports avoiding high-risk situations altogether, inquire as to how he was able to accomplish that. Explain that by not putting himself in a high-risk situation, abstinence and the positive benefits that go along with it are much more likely. Emphasize the point that when coping skills are used, results are likely to be positive, and the outcome will be a sense of confidence and a feeling of accomplishment and success. In addition, emphasize that any situation that is handled without using is an achievement and something that will make him feel more able to rely on himself without needing to use. The point to emphasize to the client is that alcohol or other drugs only serve to take away from one's own personal strengths and resources. Adolescents can readily identify with the need to feel independent, so the clinician can use this frame of reference to support the notion that the client has been relying on the substance to do what he can do for himself.

For example, the clinician might give feedback such as the following:

You told me that you and your friends just decided to rent movies on Friday instead of going to hang out at [the local party spot]. **Sounds like you were using a few different coping skills.**

First, you avoided a high-risk situation for using by making the decision to stay home and watch movies. So that's called avoidance, and you made that decision. Second, you and your friends found an enjoyable activity to do in renting some good movies. I bet that you probably had a really good time doing that, too. That's called increasing pleasant activities. And not only did you avoid using and have a good time as well, but you avoided some possible trouble you may have fallen into, like being in a car with someone who's using, or waking up the next day feeling awful, or getting caught by the police. Can you see how doing all of these things in combination helped you?

Following this discussion, the clinician then proceeds to inquire about any upcoming high-risk situations, offering ideas on how the client will apply coping skills in those situations. The clinician should always be sure to check with the client about his ideas on what coping skills to use in high-risk situations, and how to use them.

Discuss a relapse prevention plan to use until the next contact.

Next, discuss a relapse prevention plan with the client that she can use until the next contact. Summarize the skills that have been working well and ask the client how likely it is that she will be able to continue using those skills. Additionally, summarize any new suggestions made to apply coping skills in the future.

Encourage the client to make an effort, even though it might seem difficult at times. Also, encourage the client not to forget about the negative consequences of her use and emphasize the reasons she feels the need to become abstinent or reduce use. Continue to use an empathic and supportive style throughout the call. For example:

> **So we talked about how you've been able to stay clean. Can you see yourself continuing to incorporate those skills into your life as time progresses?**
>
> **Are there any upcoming high-risk situations that you can foresee where you'll need to pay close attention to things?**
>
> **What skills do you think you'll need to emphasize the most in upcoming high-risk situations?** *[Or, say:]* **It sounds like you'll need to use** *[particular coping skill]* **in that situation to help offset all of those high-risk factors for you. How does that sound to you?**
>
> **Are you worried about being able to handle that situation?**
>
> **You might consider reviewing the Coping Skills Summary Sheet that I gave you at our first visit to help remind you of the things that can be helpful.**
>
> **Are there any other aspects that you can think of that will be helpful to you as you go along?**

STEP 2B ▶▶▶
Client reports substance use since last contact and is adequately motivated for change. Rated motivation is at least a 5 on a 0–10 scale.

Using a neutral, empathic tone, clinicians should begin this step by briefly assessing the client's reaction to his use:

> So you had a few occasions in the past few weeks when you drank alcohol. Looking back on those occasions, how does that feel for you now at this point? *[Listen. Comment on motivation:]* **And your motivation is at a** *[5 or above]*?

Next, the clinician proceeds with a discussion of the situations and circumstances (that is, the internal and external triggers) that prompted substance use. Use the Coping Skills Summary Sheet to help facilitate this dialogue. Process factors that seem most relevant to the client and focus on how the situation might have gone differently if coping skills had been employed before and during the high-risk situation. Encourage the client to consider using coping strategies in response to high-risk situations in the future. For example:

> **What were some of those high-risk factors that you think made it more difficult for you to stay clean?**
>
> **Sounds like that situation was really tough for you. What would you have done differently if you had tried really hard to stay clean** *[succeeded in staying clean]*?
>
> **So in the past, you used** *[a particular coping strategy]*, **but this time things were a little different. Looking back on how you handled that situation, what factors were different and how might you have done things differently?**
>
> **Can you identify coping skills that you might have focused on more that may have helped you have a different outcome?**
>
> **What do you think about the idea of focusing more on** *[suggestion for coping skill]* **the next time that high-risk situation comes up?** *[Listen.]* **How do you think you might end up thinking or feeling differently if you did that?**
>
> **If you tried to cope with those** *[internal and external triggers]* **by using** *[coping skill]*, **how do you think that might help you think and feel differently? Do you think you would be less likely to end up using?**
>
> **Using** *[coping skill]* **would involve** *[describe coping skill]*. **Do you think that it would be useful for you to try to focus on using some of those ideas when faced with a high-risk situation next time?**

Note: If the client seems to have a degree of ambivalence about the episode(s) of substance use (or the potential for more to occur), use

MI/MET strategies to address motivation/readiness to change factors. An inquiry into how the client feels about the idea of attempting abstinence at this point in time (*not* a pressured agenda) can also be useful to help keep the client focused on progress. When discussing abstinence, the clinician should strive to be accepting of any response to avoid polarizing the client. Develop discrepancy, if possible, between the client's stated goals in session 1 and current behaviors. If motivation for change seems questionable, or if ambivalence continues, the clinician may need to proceed to step 2C, which is a focus only on MI/MET style of dialogue. (Despite using the 0–10 rating scale with the client, the clinician may still need to decide what is an adequate level of motivation to proceed to a coping skills discussion versus continuing with an MI/MET approach, step 2C.) Also, it may be common to hear both types of statements from clients: a willingness to stop or reduce substance use, yet ambivalence about doing so. In such cases, a combination of approaches may be used: some coping skills discussion combined with MET language/interventions. For example:

> **A few of the ideas you listed on your goal sheet about staying clean** [making progress] **the first time we met are** [aspects listed]. **Do you think those are likely to be helpful going forward?**
>
> **And some of your other goals or visions you listed for yourself are to** [goals listed]. **Are there positive benefits for you to continue making progress?**
>
> **You said something that was important to you was** [goal listed]. **How do you think making more progress will help that come to fruition?**
>
> **It sounds like this is something that's very important to you. I give you a lot of credit. I know how difficult making progress can feel sometimes.**
>
> **I'm impressed that your motivation remains at** [X]. **Sometimes when we slip up, it can make us wonder, "What's the point?"**
>
> **So you're motivated to continue progressing—why is that so important to you?**
>
> **Do you think staying clean helps your confidence and self-esteem?**
>
> **How do other important people in your life react to times when you end up using?**

Next, the clinician briefly summarizes the discussion into a plan to employ the discussed coping skills before the next session, while encouraging the client to use the strategies discussed during difficult times. For example:

> It sounds like we've identified how things became difficult for you and how you ended up using. Let's see if we can help you develop a plan to put some of the skills we discussed into practice when those high-risk situations present themselves again. How do you think that will look?
>
> How can you incorporate those coping skills into your routine so that those high-risk situations can become low-risk situations for substance use the next time they occur?
>
> You might consider reviewing the Coping Skills Summary Sheet that I gave you at our first visit to help remind you of things that can be helpful.
>
> Can you think of any other strategies that will be helpful to you as you go along?

STEP 2C ▶▶▶
Client reports using since last contact and is inadequately motivated for change.

If the client is not adequately motivated to make changes regarding her level of use—that is, the level of motivation is below a 5—do not attempt to use coping skills material for the discussion. Rather, rely on the use of the following MI/MET techniques to address readiness for change factors. Incorporate information from the CSSA and Goal-Setting Worksheet in this dialogue to help facilitate the discussion. Do not pressure an agenda of abstinence or change. Rather, hold an open, nonjudgmental discussion about various relevant factors that play a role in the client's decision about continuing to use or not.

- Express empathy.
- Develop discrepancy.
- Avoid argumentation.
- Roll with resistance.
- Support self-efficacy.

For a detailed description and examples of MI/MET techniques, refer to the guidelines listed on pages 75–78. You may say to the client (remaining neutral and nonjudgmental, and pausing for responses):

> **So you've been using at a level of** *[X]* **since the last time we talked, and your motivation to make progress is at** *[X]*. **It sounds like you're not very interested in trying to make changes at this point. Can you tell me where you're at with that in your own mind?**
>
> **I think it's normal for people to go through times when they just don't feel like making any changes. Is that how it is for you at this point?**
>
> **I know how difficult considering change can be. Sometimes it feels like others are just pressuring you to change.**
>
> **What is it about trying to make changes that bothers you the most?**
>
> **One of the goals you talked about when we first met was** *[goal listed]*. **I'm just wondering where you're at with that right now?**
>
> **In the past, substance use has affected you in a pretty negative way. Is that right? Can you tell me more about that?**
>
> **What are some of the things you really liked when you weren't using at all** *[were using less]*?
>
> **Part of my job is to help you try to consider alternative scenarios for your life. I know it seems like substance use isn't hurting you right now, but is it okay if I ask you if it's consistent with where you see yourself being in the future?**
>
> **I think you have a lot of strengths. Some of the things you've told me that you like to do** *[are good at doing]* **are** *[X]*. **Would you say substance use contributes to or takes away from your abilities overall?**
>
> **I guess my hope for you is that somewhere inside you might consider the idea that substance use takes away from who you really are and all of the great qualities about you.**
>
> **Is it okay if I ask you how substance use has affected you negatively in the past?**

> **NOTE**
> If at *any* point during the session the client presents with an unwillingness/reticence to participate in an abstinence- or change-based discussion, MI/MET techniques may be employed.

If the client has returned to a level of more frequent and increased substance use, consider whether to make a recommendation and referral for more intensive treatment. Discuss treatment options with the client, and also discuss the case with a clinical supervisor.

STEPS 3A AND 3B ▸▸▸
Close the session if coping skills discussion has been used (or MI/MET included in discussion).

In this final step of the session, the clinician briefly summarizes the call, reiterates direct suggestions for employing coping skills, and gives generous positive feedback about the client's participation. The next session date, time, and location should be scheduled and confirmed. For example:

> **We've talked about where you're at right now in terms of substance use, your motivation to continue progressing, and some ideas that you can continue to keep in mind, especially around high-risk times. You've told me that using certain coping skills** [mention those discussed] **have helped you, and you feel that if you can implement those as you progress, you'll continue to work toward accomplishing your goals. We also talked about how you can get those skills to work for you and the positive effects of continuing to make efforts.**
>
> **You really did a great job today in participating in this session. I think this is a testament to your dedication and desire to continually improve yourself.**
>
> **So let's go ahead and schedule the next date, time, and location for the next session.**

STEP 3C ▸▸▸
Close the session if motivational enhancement techniques have been used.

Summarize the discussion and end the call by making a motivational statement that sends a message of concern for the client and hope for change. Give generous praise for taking part in the call. The next session date, time, and location should be scheduled and confirmed. For example:

> We've talked about the process of change relative to where you're at right now in terms of substance use. My hope for you is that as time goes along, you'll become more aware of how substance use has the potential to take away from all of your natural gifts and talents. I also hope that talking openly like you did today can help you realize how the choices you make now can really affect what happens later for you.
>
> Thanks for participating in this session today. You really gave honest input about how this process is progressing for you.
>
> So let's go ahead and schedule the next date, time, and location for the next session.

The Aftercare Post-Session Summary Sheet

Following each of the aftercare sessions 2 through 5, the clinician completes the Aftercare Post-Session Summary Sheet. Then, just prior to each of the following contacts, the clinician reviews this information so that he is updated on the content of the previous sessions.

Additions to Session 5 of Aftercare

In the final contact of this aftercare program, additional dialogue is added to the end of the session. Included in step 3, the clinician should cover termination issues with the client. Material to cover during this portion of the session includes:

- ▸ a brief review of the client's progress over the course of the previous twelve weeks
- ▸ a summary of where the clinician feels the client is in the process of achieving and/or maintaining stated goals

- a recommendation to the client regarding a course of action with further treatment
- continued use of coping skills in high-risk situations
- a motivational statement for continued change

Referrals and recommendations for other issues that may require treatment (such as family problems or depression) should also be given if necessary.

Appendixes

Appendix 1

How the Program Works: A Case Vignette

The following is a practical demonstration of the program:

Paul is a fifteen-year-old who was using marijuana daily. He was arrested with a friend for possession of half an ounce of marijuana and drug paraphernalia. He was mandated to substance abuse outpatient treatment by the court system. During treatment, Paul admitted to smoking pot daily and to weekend alcohol use. He was able to make progress during the course of treatment, and he reduced his use of marijuana significantly. However, he has begun to use alcohol more frequently. Paul completed twelve sessions of outpatient AOSUD treatment and agreed to participate in five sessions of aftercare over the following twelve weeks.

Paul is transitioned to an aftercare clinician, whom he meets with in person for an initial session. Paul's aftercare clinician reviews the Transition to Aftercare Form (TAF) for background information regarding his level of substance use and other clinical issues. In session 1, the clinician helps Paul identify high-risk situations and triggers that are still contributing to substance use (CBT awareness strategies). Paul verbalizes his ambivalence about quitting drug and alcohol use "for good." Goals that Paul is interested in accomplishing in the short term are discussed and written down (Goal-Setting Worksheet). Negative consequences of using and positive benefits of abstinence are discussed, as are high-risk situations for alcohol and drug use. Specific coping skills Paul can use to help increase his confidence in his ability to abstain from drug use in high-risk situations are addressed. The clinician maintains a nonjudgmental stance, letting Paul "decide" whether he would like to incorporate those skills to achieve his goals (combination of MET and CBT).

The next three aftercare sessions are conducted over the telephone with Paul. The clinician uses information discussed in each prior session (which is summarized on the Aftercare Post-Session Summary Sheet), reported substance use, and motivation factors as a guide for the dialogue. The length of these sessions is fifteen minutes. Paul continues to reduce the frequency of his substance use episodes, and he feels proud that he's barely using at all. He's been able to identify the high-risk situations that still present challenges for him, and he has developed a more productive set of coping mechanisms to handle these situations. The clinician provides an ongoing supportive stance toward Paul at all times. Success is rewarded with praise, while slips/substance use episodes are framed as learning experiences, emphasizing the "process" nature of growing out of using drugs and alcohol as a coping mechanism. New thoughts and behaviors in relation to substance use prevention occur through teaching, coaching, motivating, empathy, and positive regard. Paul's self-efficacy to remain sober continues to expand.

Paul attends his final session of aftercare in person. In this session, Paul admits to a recent episode of heavier marijuana use. Paul remains highly motivated to continue doing well. He and the clinician process his episode of heavy use, identifying the high-risk situation and triggers present. Paul is reminded of his success thus far, the negative consequences he's managed to avoid, and the positive benefits he's experienced. The two discuss how Paul could have managed the episode with increased coping skills. Paul is informed that he'll continue to be faced with high-risk situations for substance use, but that he can continue to rely on himself to incorporate productive coping skills. Paul is encouraged to call in the future if he needs a referral for more treatment, and the aftercare treatment ends.

Appendix 2

Progression of Sessions

These examples show how a progression of sessions 2 through 5, conducted via telephone, might proceed with a client. John and his clinician have completed the first in-person session of aftercare and are now ready to begin aftercare sessions 2 through 5.

J = John; C = Clinician

Sample Script for Session 2

C: Hi, John, this is Sarah from [clinic name]**. Is this an okay time to talk? Do you have enough privacy right now?**

J: Yeah, hold on a minute. I'll be right back. . . . Okay, I'm good now.

C: So, we met about two weeks ago for the first session of aftercare, right?

J: Yeah, I guess it was about two weeks ago.

C: Just to remind you, today is our first telephone session out of a total of four, and we'll be talking for about fifteen minutes or so, okay?

J: Sure.

C: How have you been doing since we met two weeks ago?

J: Good. I just finished moving.

C: Oh yeah, that's right. I remember that you were telling me that the last time we met. How did the move go?

J: It went good; I had a few friends help me out with moving everything.

C: And you moved in with your father, right?

J: Yeah.

C: I assume that's a good thing for you?

J: Yeah. I'm really stressed right now, though, 'cause my mom's in the hospital.

C: Oh, wow, I'm sorry to hear that. Is she okay?

J: Yeah, she's okay. She's having some tests done today, I think.

C: Well, I hope everything goes okay for her.

J: Thanks.

C: Let's talk about how you've been doing in terms of substance use since the last time we talked. Have you used alcohol or other drugs at all over the past two weeks?

J: Yeah. I drank a few times. Nothing else, though.

C: Okay, so you drank on a few occasions. How many times total in the past two weeks did you have something to drink?

J: I guess it was like twice on the weekends, when I was hanging out with a few of my friends.

C: So that was the situation? You were hanging out with your friends. How much did you have to drink on each occasion?

J: I guess it was like about six or seven beers each time. I was pretty drunk.

C: Okay, so you drank on two occasions, each time about six or seven beers. I'm looking at what you reported drinking the last time we met, and that looks to be about the same as you had been doing before. You reported drinking on average about once a week, anywhere from five to ten drinks.

J: Yeah, that sounds about right.

C: Before we talk more in detail about that, let me just ask you about your motivation. How would you rate your motivation to make a change in your drinking behavior at this point, on a scale of 0 to 10, with 0 being no motivation and 10 being the most motivation you could have?

J: I guess I would say it's about a 6 right now.

C: Okay, so your motivation to change is still the same as you reported when we met for our first in-person session, is that right?

J: Yeah. Nothing's changed, really.

C: Did you use any other drugs over the past two weeks?

J: No, I don't really do anything else besides drink. I used to smoke pot once in a while, but I don't really do that anymore.

C: Okay, good. Is it okay if we talk in more detail about the days when you drank alcohol during the past two weeks?

J: Sure, why not?

C: Tell me what kinds of situations you were in. You said you were hanging out with your friends—were you guys at a party, or just at someone's house, or somewhere else?

J: We usually hang out at my friend Steve's house. His parents are cool; they don't really bother us, so we just hang out in his basement. It's cool down there—he's got a big screen and a pool table, so it's fun.

C: Oh, yeah, I remember you talking about Steve's house last time. There are several of you that usually hang out together, right?

J: Yeah, there's a bunch of us. We all kind of like doing the same things, so it's cool.

C: And do your friends all drink, too?

J: Yeah, they all drink, except for Mike. He doesn't like to drink, but he'll smoke a little weed sometimes.

C: Okay, so that's the typical high-risk situation for you then, hanging out at your friend Steve's house, right?

J: Yeah. I mean, there are some other times when I drink, too, but usually that's, like, the main time.

> C: Right. So, I'm looking at your goal sheet from our last meeting and reviewing some of the reasons you said that you wanted to make a change in your drinking. Can you remember what you were telling me from the first session as to what your goals are?

J: Yeah, I know one of the things I said was that I want to be able to just have like one or two beers once in a while, and not always get so carried away with it. Seems like every time I drink I end up getting, like, really drunk.

> C: Yeah, that was the goal you came up with. And why is that important to you? I mean, why make that a goal?

J: Well, 'cause when I get drunk, I do stupid things sometimes and end up getting in trouble. That's how I ended up in the program to begin with. I got arrested for bringing alcohol to school and being drunk on school grounds.

> C: Right. I remember you telling me that story. So you want to be able to drink once in a while, but only have one or two beers. It sounds like you have really good reasons why you want to make a change. You're tired of getting in trouble because of things that you do when you drink a lot. Are there any other reasons you want to make a change?

J: Well, I know my parents don't really trust me and stuff, and so it's like they're always checking up on me. I'm just tired of hearing them yell at me and stuff. And I was starting to drink, like, all the time. Like, I was sneaking it in my room when I'd be grounded. I would just lock the door and have a few shots, then call my girlfriend or something. But she was starting to get mad at me, too, 'cause I was drinking all the time.

> C: Wow, it sounds like there are several really good reasons for you to want to make a change in your drinking. And it sounds like you've made some really good progress so far; you're not drinking as much as you were.

J: Yeah, I've definitely cut back from where I was.

> C: I'm a little surprised, though, that your goal isn't to stop drinking completely, at least for a while. I say that because I'm wondering how hard it must be to try to stop drinking after having just one or two. What do you think? Have you been able to do that before?

J: Sometimes. Like, there are times when I don't really drink at all, even if I'm with my friends. We'll all be hanging out and doing something else, shooting hoops or something like that.

> C: Oh, wow, that's great. So there are times when you guys all get together and do something else that's really enjoyable, like playing basketball. Great!

J: Yeah, but I mean, we get bored, too, sometimes. There just isn't really anything else going on, so we just hang out and drink, you know?

> C: Yeah. But I'm still wondering how you'll be able to get yourself to drink just one or two and be able to stop, especially when your friends are still drinking.

J: I know it's going to be hard to do that. I guess I'll just have to try it and see what happens.

> C: What I'm getting at here, John, is whether just having one or two beers is a realistic expectation for yourself. I mean, it seems like a total setup for you in some ways. See, what happens is the more times you try to do something and fail at it, the less you believe you can actually do it, so you might just end up giving up on it altogether, you know?

J: Yeah, I know what you mean, 'cause I've been saying this to myself for a while now, and it's, like, not really working.

> C: Oh, okay. You're starting to realize that there's a part of you that has the desire to only have a few drinks, but then once you start drinking, it's really tough to do that. That's a really great awareness to have, John. So, you know that you want to make a change in your drinking, and you have really good reasons for doing that, but it's tough to remember all of that—to stay motivated, I mean, once you've actually started drinking. Does that sound right?

J: Yeah, that's pretty much it, I guess. I mean, I kind of like drinking, too, though, you know? I don't know if I really want to just stop altogether.

> C: Sure—it's normal to feel that way, especially about something like alcohol. I mean, if it didn't feel good to your brain, you wouldn't feel conflicted about it, and we wouldn't be having this conversation right now, right?

J: That's true.

> C: So, how can we help you avoid all of these negative consequences of drinking? I mean, what's a realistic approach?

J: Maybe I shouldn't drink at all for a while.

> C: Well, you could surely try doing that. I'll support you 100 percent on that one. We could talk about some strategies you could use to help yourself do that, because it's probably going to be really tough for you to try to do that, especially at first, you know?

J: Yeah, I know.

> C: But you said that there are times when you are in the same high-risk situation with your friends, and you don't drink, so that tells me that you definitely can do it.

J: Yeah, but those times, it's like we're all not drinking; we're doing something else.

> C: Oh, right. So it sounds like you have an understanding that there are certain triggers that happen that make it more likely that you are going to end up drinking versus not drinking.

J: Yeah, like not having anything else to do. We get, like, bored really easily.

> C: So, there are a few things I'm thinking right now about those triggers. One thing is, do you remember that we talked about the idea of *increasing pleasant activities*? You know, I mean finding other really enjoyable things to do during times when you might be likely to drink.

J: Yeah, but that's the problem. Drinking is so much easier than, like, having to find something to do, and it makes things, like, seem so much more fun.

> C: Oh, okay, so that's another aspect that you just mentioned, too—that things seem to be much more fun when you are drinking. Is that right?

J: Well, yeah, definitely.

> C: Okay, so I'm going to challenge that thought a little bit here, because that's exactly what happens over time when people start to get used to using a drug like alcohol. They start to form beliefs inside about what it does for their lives. And that's a bit of a danger zone, because it's like the alcohol is starting to have a certain power over you, making you believe that "it" is the preferred way to be. It becomes like a coping mechanism. Does that make sense?

J: Well, yeah, but it does make you feel good.

> C: Of course! It's a drug that has powerful effects on the brain. But the danger is that it starts to fool you into thinking that you need it to exist, at times. Like, without it you just aren't the same person. Is that true, John? Does alcohol make you a better person?

J: No, it doesn't make me a better person. If that was the case, I wouldn't be having some of the problems I'm having because of it.

> C: Exactly. So getting back to having some other really enjoyable things to do: The idea is to sort of retrain the brain that it doesn't need alcohol to feel good, or to cope with feeling bad, for that matter. Because when you're bored, that doesn't feel good, right?

J: No, I hate being bored.

> C: Right, so you're brain is telling you something: In that instance, it needs you to find something interesting and fun to do. Do you remember the session we had on *problem solving*—you know, the one that helped you define what a problem is, then break it down into parts and generate different ideas about solutions?

J: Yeah, I remember a little of that.

> C: So, for a moment, try to think of this situation as a problem to be solved. If you were to brainstorm ideas about interesting and fun things to do besides drinking, what do you think you'd come up with?

J: Well, we all like sports, shooting hoops. And we like video games, and playing poker, too. But when we're at Steve's house, it's like we can do those things and drink, too, you know?

> C: Right. So how about adding the idea of hanging out at a different location, like at your house, or one of the other guy's houses? Is that something you think you could suggest to your friends?

J: Yeah. I don't know how it'd go over, but I could try it.

> C: You could also add the idea of being *assertive* here when talking with your friends about this. I mean, you could let them know that you're trying to stop drinking and tell them you have some ideas about doing different things instead.

J: Well, because Phil is so getting himself in trouble, it's like all he's doing is drinking. He really needs to stop.

> C: So you could be the one to suggest something different. And you said Mike doesn't really drink, either, so you could maybe use him as a supporter of your idea. What do you think?

J: I could try it, I guess.

> C: Okay, great! So, we talked about a lot of different ideas today, John. We talked about the high-risk situation that sets you up to drink. And we talked about your goal and the negative consequences drinking is having on your life, the idea of abstinence versus just trying to reduce your drinking, and some different coping strategies to help you. You've got some really clear understanding about this whole situation. I have to tell you, I'm really impressed with you. You're a pretty mature guy for your age.

J: I'm trying.

> C: Okay, so any questions before we end the call for today?

J: No, I think I'm good for now.

>C: **Great. We'll be talking again in about two weeks. Can I call you right at the same time in two weeks?**

J: Sure, that's fine.

>C: **Great. Well, thanks for talking with me today. You did a great job, and I'll look forward to hearing how things go for you over the next few weeks. Good luck!**

J: Thanks.

Sample Script for Session 3

>C: **Hi, is this John?**

J: Hi, Sarah.

>C: **John, is this an okay time for the call?**

J: Sure, it's fine. There's nobody home now, so this is a good time.

>C: **Great. Just as a reminder, this is our third contact in this aftercare program so far. How have things been for you since we talked two weeks ago?**

J: They're going okay, I guess. My parents have been really getting on my nerves lately, though. I'm actually grounded right now.

>C: **Oh, wow, sorry to hear that. What happened?**

J: Take a guess . . .

>C: **Hmmm, let me see. You got caught drinking?**

J: Yep, you got it.

>C: **Yikes, so I guess you're in trouble. Before we get into that, let me just check to see how you've done in the past two weeks with your drinking. How many days in the past two weeks did you have something to drink?**

J: Well, I was doing good until this past weekend, then I got totally wasted at Steve's house on Saturday, and I came home and puked all over my bed. That's how my father found out.

>C: **So was that the only day you drank in the past two weeks?**

J: Yeah. I actually tried not to drink anything the rest of the time, but I just gave in on Saturday. My father was really pissed at me, and of course he had to tell my mother. Then she went off on me, too.

> C: Wow. Well, I'm glad to hear that you were able to stay sober on those other days. Tell me: Right now, where would you say your motivation is to not drink on that 0–10 scale?

J: Well, right now it's, like, pretty high, 'cause now I'm grounded for the next week. Probably like an 8, I guess.

> C: Oh, so you mean that getting into trouble with your parents because of being drunk on Saturday has increased your motivation?

J: Kind of. I mean I was, like, actually trying, and then I just gave in on Saturday, so I feel kind of stupid, you know?

> C: Sure, I can understand how you must feel. Before we talk about that, though, tell me, how were you able to stay sober on those other days? Were you doing anything differently, or did you try to use some of the suggestions we came up with the last time we talked?

J: Yeah, on one day, we all actually hung out at my house for a change. It was cool, my father let my friends come over, and we played video games for a few hours. We didn't even talk about drinking. I wasn't even thinking about it.

> C: That's great! So you tried to do something different, and it worked. That's awesome. Great job with that.

J: Yeah, except now I just ruined everything, and I'm right back where I started with both my parents not trusting me.

> C: Hmm, I see. So how did it feel to have some success on those days when you weren't drinking?

J: It felt good, like I could actually do it and it wasn't really a big deal.

> C: Great, so you felt like you were able to do something that resulted in a change. And you said you didn't even think or talk about drinking—why was that, do you think?

J: Well, I think we were just having fun doing what we were doing.

> C: You mean you guys were all hanging out enjoying yourselves without drinking? Wow! I know that's one of the beliefs I challenged you on the last time we were talking—the idea that alcohol doesn't make you any more able to have a good time.

J: Yeah, but then Saturday rolled around.

> C: And what happened? What was the situation that triggered you to drink on Saturday?

J: Well, my father let me go out, we were at Steve's, and one of the guys had a big bottle of vodka. I was just gonna have, like, one shot, and they talked me into playing a drinking game. Next think I knew, I was wasted.

> C: That was a huge setup for you. Just like we talked about last time, you had the motivation before you started drinking, but once you started, that was all gone, right?

J: Yep, that's it. Now I'm basically right back where I was a few months ago.

> C: Really? Because I would challenge that thought. You had several days in the past two weeks when you didn't drink. And you used the strategies we talked about last time to do that. Don't forget about that, John. Drinking on one day doesn't take those other successes away, right?

J: Yeah, I guess so, but try telling my father that.

> C: Well, this is a good opportunity for you to reflect on the negative consequences of your drinking again, right?

J: I'll say. I was sick for, like, two days because of Saturday. I'm just starting to feel better today. I hate that.

> C: Right. So, the idea is to learn from this by remembering how bad you are feeling now because of your drinking, and to reflect on that before the next time you go into a high-risk situation.

J: I know. I wish I could do that.

C: You *can* do that, John. It just takes a little practice to get yourself to think ahead. It's just like in the *problem-solving model*, where we talk about weighing the pros and the cons of the decisions we make before we make them. It's the same idea as preparing yourself before going into a high-risk situation. You spend a few minutes thinking about the negative consequences of drinking and the positive benefits of staying abstinent.

J: I'll be able to do that better now, I bet.

C: Great. So, we reviewed some coping skills that worked well for you today and talked about the high-risk situation that set you up to have a drinking episode and experience those negative consequences again. I would encourage you to continue to think about all of this over the next two weeks. Do you think you might be able to give those things some thought from time to time?

J: Yeah, I'm just stuck in the house now, anyway.

C: Well, why don't we stop here for today, then? Thanks for talking with me today. You're doing a really good job talking about things in these phone calls. Our next session will be in another two weeks. Is it okay if I call you at the same time?

J: Sure.

C: Great. Take care and good luck over the next few weeks!

Sample Script for Session 4

C: Hello, John. This is Sarah. How are you today?

J: I'm doing pretty good.

C: John, is this an okay time for you to talk? Do you have privacy right now?

J: Yeah, it's cool. I'm in my room.

C: Great, so today is our fourth contact. How's life been treating you in the two weeks since we talked last?

J: Things have been good. I've been avoiding the beers, haven't had anything to drink at all, so that part's been good.

C: Awesome job. That's great! Congratulations!

J: Thanks. It's been pretty easy, though. I think I really learned my lesson after last time. I'm just kind of not doing it now, and it's no big deal.

C: Wow, that's really good for you, John. Before we go further, let me ask you about your motivation. How would you rate your motivation to stay abstinent right now on a scale of 0 to 10, where 0 is no motivation and 10 is the most you could have?

J: I'd say it's pretty high, still up there, like maybe an 8 or so.

C: Great. It sounds like you're still thinking that the benefits of staying abstinent are more important than drinking; is that right?

J: Yeah, for now anyway. You never know what's going to happen, though.

C: Well, tell me how you've been staying sober for the past two weeks.

J: I was grounded, so I wasn't doing anything, and then this past weekend, I didn't really hang out with the boys. I could've gone over to Steve's, but I wasn't really into it. I just hung out at my girlfriend's house instead.

C: That's great. So you completely avoided the high-risk situation of being at Steve's house; is that right?

J: Pretty much. I mean, I knew those guys would be drinking, and I just didn't feel like doing that.

C: And how did you come to that conclusion, John?

J: I just thought about what was going to happen. I mean, I just got off being grounded, and I don't want to go through that whole thing again.

C: You mean you thought ahead about the negative consequences? That's awesome! How did you feel about making that choice?

J: I was cool with it. I had a good time with my girlfriend. We just hung out and watched movies with some of her friends. It was cool.

C: So you mean you had a good time doing that?

J: Yeah, I did. We watched a few really cool horror flicks.

C: Sounds scary. And you didn't need to drink to have fun; is that right?

J: No, I didn't even think about it. It's like when I'm not with the guys, it's not really a big deal, you know?

C: Oh, I see. You're really starting to realize, then, that the greatest high-risk time for you to drink is when you're hanging out with your friends at Steve's house. That's exactly what we talked about right from the start. Well, I think it's awesome that you were able to get yourself to consider the consequences before making a choice about what you were going to do. Do you give yourself credit for that?

J: Yeah, I guess so.

C: No, really, I think you should give yourself credit. I mean, you're the one who made that decision. No one else could decide that for you. I think that's a huge part of realizing how the choices you make affect your life and that you are the one who has the power to decide the direction things will go for you. That *problem-solving model* really helps us make very informed choices. What do you think?

J: Yeah, I actually thought about that, believe it or not. Not for long, but it did occur to me.

C: That's really great. I'm really impressed with your maturity level. And you've been really open with me through this whole process. That says a lot about you as a person, you know?

J: Well, you're pretty cool to talk to, and you don't really judge anything I'm telling you, like my parents do.

C: Okay, so tell me, are there any high-risk situations that you'll be faced with between now and the next time we talk?

J: Nah, I think this is gonna be pretty easy from now on.

C: Well, let me just challenge that thought for a moment, John. One of the toughest parts of maintaining your progress is having the ongoing awareness that you could be faced with a high-risk situation at any time. It's kind of like, as soon as you start thinking it'll be easy, that's when you become vulnerable to having it sneak up on you again.

J: Yeah, but I don't have to, like, walk around always thinking about it, right?

C: You don't necessarily have to do that, John. The idea is to have a plan in place should you be faced with a high-risk situation so that you know ahead of time how you're going to respond. Let's say, for example, that you do end up hanging out at Steve's house this weekend and the guys are drinking. How will you respond when they offer you a beer?

J: I guess I'll just tell them, "No, I'm all set."

C: And do you think that will work? I mean, do you think they'll just lay off once you tell them that?

J: Steve and Phil always like to get me doing shots, so they might not stop.

C: It sounds like you might have to be a little more assertive with them. What do you think?

J: Well, they know what happened the last time, so I'm sure they won't be, like, forcing me or anything.

C: Do you think you'll have to remind them why you're choosing not to drink?

J: Yeah, that might help.

C: Great. I would also encourage you to spend some time thinking about what you would say to them if that ends up happening. That way, you'll be totally prepared should you find yourself in that situation again. Know what I mean?

J: Yeah, 'cause I don't want to screw up again.

C: Exactly. So, today, we talked more about certain coping skills that will really help you, John, like planning ahead, being assertive with your friends, and continually reminding yourself of the negative consequences of drinking. And your motivation to maintain abstinence is high, so that's great. So, it will be three weeks until we talk again. Is it okay if I call you around the same time?

J: Sure, that's fine.

C: Great. Thanks for talking with me today, John, and take care!

Sample Script for Session 5

C: Hi, John. This is Sarah. Is this an okay time for you to talk?

J: Sure, it's fine.

C: Great. Do you have privacy to talk?

J: Yeah. I'm in my room, so it's cool.

C: Okay. Well, this is our last session of aftercare treatment. Can you believe it went by so quickly?

J: Yeah, it seems like we just started.

C: So it's been three weeks since we last talked. How have things been going for you since then?

J: Well, school's almost over, so that's good. My parents have been a lot better with me.

C: Oh, really? That's great. Before we talk more about that, let me just check in with you on your progress. Did you drink alcohol at all since we last talked?

J: Well, don't get pissed at me . . .

C: I promise I won't. You can be totally open with me, John.

J: I had, like, one beer, but then I stopped as soon as I drank it. I knew I just didn't want to end up smashed again.

C: Wow! That's great, John. You mean you were actually able to get yourself to stop drinking after having one beer? How did you do that?

J: Well, I didn't really want to drink at all, but Steve's older brother was hanging out with us, and we were all, like, trying to be cool around him, so I kinda felt stupid saying I didn't want a beer.

C: Oh, I see, so that's what happened. What did you do?

J: Well, I had one. But then I knew as soon as I did that I was just gonna get hammered again, so I bolted.

C: You did what?

J: I took off. I got out of there.

C: John, that's great. You decided to leave the situation. That must have taken a lot of guts. What did your friends say?

J: They were cool. I just told them I had a date with my girlfriend. They told me I was whipped, but I didn't care about that.

C: I am so impressed with that, John. You totally took responsibility for yourself. And you thought about the negative consequences while you were actually in the high-risk situation. That's a really tough thing to do. Congratulations!

J: Yeah, I felt pretty proud of myself afterward. I thought you were going to be pissed at me though, you know?

C: John, you did a great job, and again it's all about what you want for your life, not how anyone else judges you. You are the one who got yourself to think differently in that situation, and it resulted in you making a great choice for yourself. And then you felt really good about it later.

J: Yeah, I felt like I actually did something right for a change, instead of being a screw-up.

C: And how is your motivation to continue to not drink on that scale of 0 to 10?

J: After that day, it's pretty high, like a 9 or a 10, because I feel like I can really do it this time. Before, I don't think I really felt like I was taking myself very seriously.

C: Well, I'm really proud of you for making that choice for yourself. And it sounds like this time you really did give yourself the credit you deserved. That's really great, John.

> **So as you go forward then, without the support of the program, what kinds of things do you think you'll need to stay aware of and keep doing for yourself?**

J: Well, I know now that I can't drink at all, 'cause once I start, forget it. And I know that being at Steve's with the guys is the biggest problem for me, 'cause alcohol being there is a given. So I guess I'll just have to keep those things in mind. I just can't put myself in those situations anymore. And I'm on a pretty good roll here. I haven't, like, really screwed up in a while, and my father said he was going to take me to a baseball game if I keep on doing good.

> **C: That's awesome. So not drinking is really starting to pay off for you. It sounds like your father really notices that you're doing better, and that feels good to you. So if you can continue to get yourself to focus on all those positive benefits of not drinking and all of the negative consequences that have happened in the past because of your drinking, I think you're going to do really well for yourself.**

J: I hope so. I don't want to go backward.

> **C: All you have to do is keep doing what you're doing. Use those coping skills we talked about, think ahead, problem-solve, do other really enjoyable things, and make plans for those high-risk times. Do you think you'll be able to do that, John, to keep those skills in mind as you go forward?**

J: Yeah, I think I will. I mean, it's pretty simple stuff, really.

> **C: Does it feel like it's become easier for you to do those things over the past several weeks?**

J: Well, I kind of just got used to thinking that way, so it feels normal now. At first I didn't really think it would work.

> **C: Yeah, well, remember, alcohol is a powerful drug, and it can trick us into thinking negatively sometimes. And the more we focus on thinking that we can't do it, that it's too hard or won't work, the more we're likely to feel that way, right?**

J: Yeah, I know that now. I wish my friend Phil would do this. He's getting totally out of control.

C: Maybe you can talk with him about getting some help. Let us know if you need some referrals for him. Speaking of which, since this is our last time talking, where do you think you're at with treatment at this point? Do you think that it would be helpful for you to continue to talk to a clinician as time goes on?

J: No, not really. I think I'll be good for a while now.

C: Okay, well, just know that if you do ever decide that you would like a referral, you can call us, and we'll help you out with that, okay?

J: Okay, sure.

C: Well, John, it's been a real pleasure working with you. You really put in great effort and made some really solid choices for yourself. You have a lot to be proud of and should feel confident that you can go through these high-risk times making good, informed choices for yourself, especially now that you've incorporated those coping skills into your life.

J: I think so, yeah.

C: Well, you take care of yourself, and feel free to give me a call at any time if you feel you need some more help with this, okay?

J: Thanks.

Appendix 3

The Five Main MET Strategies

1. **Express empathy and acceptance:**
   - "Sounds like you're kinda worried about that."
   - "I can definitely understand how hard this is for you."
   - "Wow, that really was a high-risk situation."
   - "Sounds like you were really feeling down that day."

2. **Develop discrepancy:** Help the client describe the discrepancy between where he is now and where he would like to be in the future.
   - "You're saying that some things in your life might be better if you stopped using alcohol and drugs. Tell me about that."
   - "You'd like to buy a new video game, but a lot of your money is going to drugs. Tell me some more about that."
   - "Tell me how things were for you when you were clean for those two months."

3. **Avoid argumentation:** Treat ambivalence as normal, and explore it openly using double-sided reflections. If the client starts to argue with you or becomes defensive, this is a cue to modify your approach.

- "Part of you wants to quit drinking, but you're worried that you'll miss it too much."
- "I understand that you're not sure whether you want to quit. You've told me a lot of things that you like about using. It makes sense that you might not want to give that up."

4. **Roll with resistance:** Don't get rattled when the client says something against the possibility of change. Often your best response is an expression of empathy, along with either a request to hear more of her perspective and/or a slightly hopeful statement.
    - "You're saying that it seems like life would suck without getting high. Tell me some more about that."
    - "You're telling me that you have no interest in treatment. I appreciate the fact that you are speaking openly to me, and I hope that our contact meeting will be helpful to you in some way."
    - "It sounds like you feel like nothing is ever going to help you. I've seen other guys who've been in a similar spot in their lives, and I know it must be hard to hear that I think it is possible that things could get better for you."

5. **Support self-efficacy:** Reinforce any expression of willingness to hear information from you, to acknowledge the problem(s), and/or to take steps toward change. Make the connection between previous successful change and the potential to change the current problem.
    - "You're opening up about some difficult stuff."
    - "I respect your honesty about your drinking. I know it's probably not easy to talk about this."

Appendix 4

Additional MET Guidelines

Use open-ended questions and statements inviting elaboration. This keeps clients talking about the topic.

- "How do you see the situation?"
- "Tell me about your drug use."
- "Please say some more about that."

Affirm the client. Express understanding and appreciation of what the client has been going through.

- "You have been trying so hard to keep it all together, and you feel like it's all come apart."

Elicit self-motivational statements. Ask questions and make comments that encourage the client to tell you why change is desirable, rather than trying to convince the client yourself.

- "You're saying that maybe you should stop using drugs and alcohol. How come?"
- "If you were to make more progress, in what ways do you think it could help you?"

Offer feedback. When the client appears at least somewhat open to it, offer feedback of your observations or ideas in a nonjudgmental manner.

- "You've been telling me about doing more and more drugging and drinking this spring, like trying ecstasy, snorting your friend's Ritalin, and getting so drunk last weekend. I'm concerned that you may be putting your life and your health in danger."

Use reframing. Take something that at first glance sounds negative, then find and state an encouraging aspect of it, or help the client to see the risk in something she has viewed as neutral or positive.

- "Sounds like your mom is getting on your nerves, screaming and yelling about the drugs. Could it be that she's really concerned about you, but not good at expressing it?"
- "You've been able to mix a lot of drugs and alcohol, and you haven't had a situation where you've had to go to the emergency room or even might have died. Even though you feel pretty good about that, I'm concerned that it puts you at higher risk of pushing the limits to the point that something really bad *does* happen to you. What do you think?"

References

American Society of Addiction Medicine. 2001. *ASAM patient placement criteria for the treatment of substance-related disorders*. 2nd ed. rev. Chevy Chase, MD: American Society of Addiction Medicine.

Annis, H. M. 1987. Situational Confidence Questionnaire (SCQ-39). Toronto: Addiction Research Foundation.

Annis, H. M., C. S. Davis, R. K. Hester, and W. R. Miller. 1989. *Handbook of alcoholism treatment approaches*. New York: Pergamo.

Baker, R. C., C. J. Schubert, K. A. Kirwan, S. M. Lenkauskas, and J. T. Spaeth. 1999. After-hours telephone triage and advice in private and nonprivate pediatric populations. *Archive of Pediatric Adolescent Medicine* 153:292–96.

Breslin, C., L. C. Sobell, M. B. Sobell, G. Buchan, and E. Kwan. 1996. Aftercare telephone contacts with problem drinkers can serve a clinical and research function. *Addiction* 91:1359–64.

Brown, S. A., M. G. Myers, M. A. Mott, and P. W. Vik. 1994. Correlates of success following treatment for adolescent substance abuse. *Applied and Preventive Psychology* 3:61–73.

Brown, S. A., P. W. Vik, V. Creamer. 1989. Characteristics of relapse following adolescent substance abuse treatment. *Addictive Behaviors* 14:291–300.

Burleson, J., and Y. Kaminer. 2005. Adolescent substance use disorders: Self-efficacy as a predictor of relapse. *Addictive Behaviors* 20:1751–64.

Burleson, J., and Y. Kaminer. 2007. Aftercare for adolescent alcohol use disorders: Feasibility and acceptability of a phone intervention. *American Journal on Addictions* 16:202–5.

Burleson, J., Y. Kaminer, and R. Burke. 2009. Nine-month follow-up of aftercare for youth alcohol use disorders. The Annual Meeting of the Research Society on Alcoholism (RSA), San Diego, CA.

Carroll, K. M., C. Nich, and B. J. Rounsaville. 1998. Use of observer and therapist ratings to monitor delivery of coping skills treatment for cocaine abusers: Utility of therapist session checklists. *Psychotherapy Research* 8:307–20.

Carroll, K. M., C. Nich, R. L. Sifry, K. F. Nuro, T. L. Frankforter, S. A. Ball, L. Fenton, and B. J. Rounsaville. 2000. A general system for evaluating therapist adherence and competence in psychotherapy research in addictions. *Drug and Alcohol Dependence* 57:225–38.

Catanzaro, R. J., and W. G. Green. 1970. WATS telephone therapy: New follow-up technique for alcoholics. *American Journal of Psychiatry* 126:1024–27.

Corvino, J., K. Carroll, K. Nuro, C. Nich, R. Sifry, T. Frankforter, et al. 2000. Yale Adherence and Competence Scale guidelines. West Haven, CT: Yale University Psychotherapy Development Center.

Dennis, M. L., S. H. Godley, G. S. Diamond, F. M. Tims, T. Babor, J. Donaldson, H. Liddle, J. C. Titus, Y. Kaminer, C. Webb, N. Hamilton, and the CYT Steering Committee. 2004. Main findings of the Cannabis Youth Treatment (CYT) randomized field experiment. *Journal of Substance Abuse Treatment* 27:197–213.

Duncan, B. L., S. D. Miller, and J. Sparks. 2004. *The heroic client*. San Francisco: Jossey-Bass.

Godley, M. D., S. H. Godley, M. L. Dennis, R. R. Funk, and L. L. Passetti. 2007. The effect of assertive continuing care on continuing care linkage, adherence and abstinence following residential treatment for adolescents with substance use disorders. *Addiction* 102:81–93.

Gumpert, G., and S. L. Fish. 1990. *Talking to strangers: Mediated therapeutic communication*. Norwood, NJ: Ablex Publishing Corporation.

Institute of Medicine. 1990. *Broadening the base of treatment for alcohol problems*. Washington, DC: National Academy Press.

Intagliata, J. 1976. A telephone follow-up procedure for increasing the effectiveness of a treatment program for alcoholics. *Journal of Studies on Alcohol* 37:1330–1335.

Kadden, R. M., K. M. Carroll, D. M. Donovan, N. Cooney, P. Monti, D. Abrams, M. Litt, and R. Hester. 1992. *Cognitive-behavioral coping skills therapy manual: A clinical research guide for therapists treating individuals with alcohol abuse and dependence*. Rockville, MD: National Institute of Alcohol Abuse and Alcoholism.

Kaminer, Y. 1994. *Adolescent substance abuse: A comprehensive guide to theory and practice*. New York: Plenum Press.

Kaminer, Y. 2001. Adolescent substance abuse treatment: Where do we go from here? *Psychiatric Services* 52:147–49.

Kaminer, Y., and O. G. Bukstein, eds. 2008. *Adolescent substance abuse: Dual diagnosis and high-risk behaviors.* New York: Routledge/Taylor & Francis.

Kaminer, Y., J. A. Burleson, C. Blitz, J. Sussman, and B. J. Rounsaville. 1998. Psychotherapies for adolescent substance abusers. *Journal of Nervous and Mental Disease* 186:684–90.

Kaminer, Y., J. Burleson, and R. Burke. 2008. Aftercare for adolescents with alcohol use disorders: A randomized controlled study. *Journal of the American Academy of Child & Adolescent Psychiatry* 47 (12): 1405–12.

Kaminer, Y., J. Burleson, and R. Goldberger. 2002. Psychotherapies for adolescent substance abusers: Short- and long-term outcomes. *Journal of Nervous and Mental Disease* 190:737–45.

Kaminer, Y., J. Burleson, D. Goldston, and R. Burke. 2006. Suicidal ideation among adolescents with alcohol use disorders during treatment and aftercare. *American Journal of Addictions* 15 (Suppl. 1): 43–49.

Kaminer, Y., and C. Napolitano. 2004. Dial for therapy: Aftercare for adolescent substance use disorders. *Journal of the American Academy of Child & Adolescent Psychiatry* 43:1171–74.

Koumans, A. J., J. J. Muller, and C. F. Miller. 1967. Use of telephone calls to increase motivation for treatment in alcoholics. *Psychological Reports* 16:327–28.

Marlatt, G. A. 1996. Taxonomy of high-risk situations for alcohol relapse: Evolution and development of cognitive-behavioral model. *Addiction* 91:37–50.

McKay, J. R. 1999. Studies of factors in relapse to alcohol and drug use: A critical review of methodologies and findings. *Journal of Studies on Alcohol* 60:566–76.

McKay, J. R. 2001. Effectiveness of continuing care interventions for substance abusers. Implications for the study of long-term effects. *Evaluation Review* 25:211–32.

McKay, J. R., K. G. Lynch, D. S. Shepard, S. Ratichek, R. Morrison, J. Koppenhaver, and H. M. Pettinati. 2004. The effectiveness of telephone-based continuing care in the clinical management of alcohol and cocaine use disorders: 12-month outcomes. *Journal of Consulting and Clinical Psychology* 72:967–79.

McKay, J. R., A. T. McLellan, A. I. Alterman, J. S. Cacciola, M. J. Rutherford, and C. P. O'Brien. 1998. Predictors of participation in aftercare sessions and self-help groups following completion of intensive outpatient treatment for substance abuse. *Journal of Studies on Alcohol* 59:152–62.

McLellan, A. T. 2002. Have we evaluated addiction treatment correctly? Implications from a chronic care perspective. *Addiction* 97:249–55.

McLellan, A. T., C. D. Lewis, C. P. O'Brien, and H. D. Kleber. 2000. Drug dependence, a chronic medical illness: Implications for treatment. *Journal of the American Medical Association* 284:1689–95.

Miller, W. R., and S. Rollnick. 2002. *Motivational interviewing: Preparing people for change.* 2nd ed. New York: Guilford Press.

Miller, W. R., A. Zweban, C. C. DiClemente, and R. G. Rychtarik. 1992. *Motivational enhancement therapy manual: A clinical guide for therapists treating individuals with alcohol abuse and dependence.* Rockville, MD: National Institute on Alcohol Abuse and Alcoholism.

Monti, P. M., D. B. Abrams, R. M. Kadden, and N. L. Cooney. 1989. *Treating alcohol dependence: A coping skills training guide.* New York: Guilford Press.

O'Brien, C. P., and A. T. McLellan. 1996. Myths about the treatment of addiction. *Lancet* 347:237–40.

Prochaska, J. O., C. C. DiClemente, and J. C. Norcross. 1992. In search of how people change: Application to addictive behaviors. *American Psychologist* 47:1102–14.

Rutter, D. R. 1987. *Communicating by telephone.* Oxford: Pergamon Press.

Sampl, S., and R. M. Kadden. 2001. *Motivational enhancement therapy and cognitive behavioral therapy for adolescent cannabis users: 5 sessions.* Cannabis Youth Treatment Series, vol. 1. Rockville, MD: Center for Substance Abuse Treatment.

Spear, S. H., and S. Y. Skala. 1995. Posttreatment services for chemically dependent adolescents. In *Adolescent Drug Abuse: Clinical Assessment and Therapeutic Interventions*, eds. E. Rahdert and D. Czechowicz. NIDA Research Monograph, no. 156. Rockville, MD: National Institute on Drug Abuse.

Spirito, A., J. Boergers, D. Donaldson, D. Bishop, and W. Lewander. 2002. An intervention trial to improve adherence to community treatment by adolescents after a suicide attempt. *Journal of the American Academy of Child & Adolescent Psychiatry* 41 (4): 435–42.

Stout, R. L., A. Rubin, W. Zwick, et al., 1999. Optimizing the cost-effectiveness of alcohol treatment: A rationale for extended case monitoring. *Addictive Behaviors* 24 (1): 17–35.

Webb, C., M. Scudder, Y. Kaminer, R. M. Kadden. 2002. *Motivational enhancement therapy and cognitive behavioral therapy for adolescent cannabis users: 7 sessions.* Cannabis Youth Treatment Series, vol. 1. Rockville, MD: Center for Substance Abuse Treatment.

Williams, F. 1984. *The new communications.* Belmont, CA: Wadsworth.

Zhu, S. H., G. J. Tedeschi, C. M. Anderson, and J. P. Pierce. 1996. Telephone counseling for smoking cessation: What's in a call? *Journal of Counseling and Development* 75:93–100.

About the Authors

Yifrah Kaminer, M.D., M.B.A., is a Professor of Psychiatry and Pediatrics at the University of Connecticut Alcohol Research Center. Dr. Kaminer was trained as a Child and Adolescent Psychiatrist and has been conducting research on the assessment and treatment of youth substance use disorders since 1988. He is the primary author of the Teen Addiction Severity Index (T-ASI) and has authored 130 publications. His most recent books include *Adolescent Substance Abuse: Psychiatric Comorbidity and High-Risk Behaviors* (Routledge, 2008) and *A Clinical Manual of Adolescent Substance Abuse Treatment* (American Psychiatric Publishing, 2010).

Chris Napolitano, M.S., L.M.F.T., has been a full-time clinician and research associate for the University of Connecticut Health Center for the past thirteen years. He has authored several unpublished psychotherapy treatment manuals for research studies in adult and adolescent substance abuse. In addition to his clinical expertise in the delivery of psychotherapy for children, adolescents, and adults, Mr. Napolitano has conducted extensive trainings and supervision for clinicians delivering manualized research psychotherapy protocols. He has also maintained a private part-time clinical practice out of offices in the towns of Portland and Bristol, Connecticut, for the past ten years, where he utilizes both individual and systemic models of psychotherapy.